Give Us This Day...

Lenten reflections on baking bread and discipleship.

Christopher Levan

SEABURY BOOKS
an imprint of
Church Publishing Incorporated, New York

Library of Congress Cataloguing in Publication Data

Levan, Christopher, 1953-
  Give us this day : Lenten reflections on baking bread and discipleship / Christopher Levan.
     p. cm.
  ISBN-13: 978-1-59627-046-6 (pbk.)
  1. Lent--Meditations. 2. Bread. 3. Cookery (Bread) I. Title.

BV85.L48 2007
242'.34--dc22

                                                    2006033457

Cover image photographed by Mark Thomas; courtesy of Jupiter Images
Cover design by Amy Harte

Church Publishing Incorporated
445 Fifth Avenue
New York, NY 10016

Printed in the United States of America.

07 08 09 10 11 12   10 9 8 7 6 5 4 3 2 1

To: Marjory Levan, a loving cook
whose meals work their own miracles.

Christopher Levan

Author, baker, critic, journalist, pastor, and playwright, Christopher
Levan was recently appointed President and Principal of Huntington
University, Sudbury, Ontario. Previously he was well-known in the
Edmonton area as Principal of St. Stephen's College and author of a
weekly column in the *Edmonton Journal*.

He has a long experience in global peace and justice issues, as well as in
writing and research in the field of ethics. Recent publications include
Knowing Your Ethical Preferences: A Working Guide (ITP Nelson, 2000);
Living in the Maybe (Eerdmans, 1998); and *God Hates Religion* (United
Church Publishing House, 1995).

A graduate of Emmanuel College, Toronto and the Université de
Quebec, Levan holds a PhD in Systematic Theology from McGill
University. In Sudbury, he enjoys water sports, camping, skiing, and
riding with his family.

Contents

Introduction

Introduction
Give Us This Day Our Daily Bread

"Bread takes time."
By hand it's a day-long project. Even with the assistance of mechanical kitchen aids, it's still a two or three hour exercise. This is a good thing, because something happens to food when it becomes "fast." Nourishment that is prepared quickly has no soul. It satisfies our physical hunger, but leaves the spirit untouched.

"Why?" you ask. "Why not cook quickly so we have more time for 'quality moments' with those we love?"

"Ah," I reply, "Because cooking in general, and bread making in particular, is more than the intentional combination of disparate biological materials. One of the essential food groups, and one found in every healthy menu, is compassion for others."

Picture yourself at the kitchen counter. When you whisk up your latest creation, you are stirring in all your care and concerns for those who will eat this dish. (More on this later...This book is devoted to the culinary delights of the heart, so let us go slowly.)

"Bread takes time."
I'm repeating it because there is more. In the mixing, kneading, and rising, bread making has a language of its own, a dialect which cannot be understood on the fly and one not suited to designer lifestyles in the passing lane. Bread speaks to us of our daily reliance upon a Maker. Perhaps more than any other foodstuff, it brings us close to our roots as fellow creatures of God's creation. In that sense, bread is an apt metaphor for the spiritual journey.

Open any self-help devotional and you will discover that somewhere in the first chapter there is an admonition to slow down. It's not that spiritual shepherds are a lethargic lot. If you want to encounter the Creator, you have to lose the pretence of being "too busy," "too important," or "too anxious." Let this guide become your invitation to be extravagant and to lavish on your spirit untold hours of contemplation! For those of us who have to have their hands working at all times, this guide comes with a selection of recipes as well as daily devotions. So as we work our way toward Easter, we'll also be exploring the making of new breads.

The bread recipes have an added purpose. Aside from the connections made between the nature of a particular bread mixture and the journey of the soul, the recipes are designed to produce three loaves or portions: one for yourself, one for those you love, and one to give away. Any spirituality worth its salt takes us into God's presence, but doesn't leave us there. The bread of heaven—even the type Jesus mentioned—brings us back to earth. So if you follow this guide, you'll have lots of bread to give away—a practical and tangible commitment to loving this world as God does (John 3:16). Besides, imagine the circle of friends you'll create over 40 short days. They'll be lining up at your oven door, waiting to taste the results of your next devotions.

"Bread takes time."
Jesus knew that when he coined the phrase, "Give us this day our daily bread." The effort we expend in finding and shaping the nourishment we need for the day is a check against avarice. When we're busy kneading at the bread, we don't have time to hoard more than our share. Extra hours at the mixing bowl equate to fewer trips to the mall. If Jesus is calling his followers to recall the daily bread of the wilderness, manna, then central to this petition is the request to be given "enough"—neither an excess nor less than we require. So if you find the theme of sufficiency sprouting up throughout this guide, you're in the right garden patch. In fact, we could summarize Christ's innovative and revolutionary prayer with those simple words: "Give us enough."

"Enough" is a relative term. It means quite divergent things to different cultures. In some cases it's a question of material existence. In others it's a standard of social integration or spiritual well-being. Consequently, this guide explores four major dimensions of daily bread discipleship. Jesus used a shared loaf to offer (1) freedom for the fretful, (2) real food for the hungry, (3) acceptance for the outcast, and (4) empowerment for the vulnerable.

So what are we waiting for? Let's get baking!

A few notes

First, for the novice, there is a glossary at the back of this guide—definitions and helpful hints to ensure that our bread making is both a true prayer and a delicious feast. Second, most of the gospel passages used for this guide have been taken from The Scholars Version—a translation developed by the Jesus Seminar.[1] Finally, you don't have to follow the daily readings slavishly. Skip around. Find your own flow. Each day is a complete story.

---

1. The Scholars Version (SV) is found in a number of texts, but I have chosen to use *The Complete Gospels*, edited by Robert J. Miller, (Santa Rosa, CA: Polebridge Press). Copyright 1992, 1994. Used by permission.

The biblical quotation on page 27 is from the Holy Bible, New Revised Standard Version, Copyright ©1989, by the Division of Christian Education of the National Council of Churches of Christ in the United States of America. Used by permission.

A Bread Benediction

Be gentle
When you touch bread.

Let it not lie uncared for—unwanted.
So often
Bread is taken for granted.

There is so much beauty in bread:
Beauty of sun and soil,
Beauty of patient toil,
Wind and rain have caressed it,
Christ often blessed it.

Be gentle
When you touch bread.

Old Scottish Verse

First Ingredient of Daily Bread Discipleship

Don't Fret

Shrove Tuesday:
Never Fret Pancakes

Opening Prayer

Dear God, when do I have time to pray? I'm just so pressed, so much to do. Lent is starting, the pancake dinner to attend, Ash Wednesday services to...Okay, maybe I can spare a few minutes...I'm waiting...Who me? No, I don't have anything to say, well except I don't know how I'll hold everything together, keep the wagon train moving...Maybe you want to tell me something?...You do? What's that? "Slow down, don't worry so much." Easy for you to say. All right...all right. I'll try.

Matthew 6:27
"Can any of you add one hour to life by fretting about it?"

"That's it?" I'm muttering to myself, staring at the back of the premixed pancake mix box. The handy dandy instructions say that I should add melted butter, one egg, and equal measures of milk and the pancake mix.

For my mind, there is precious little "pre-mixed" in the box. So where's the saving? I suppose it is time. With the store bought variety, you can make pancakes without looking up a cook book. For the culinarily challenged, maybe it's a matter of assurance. The package says you can do it with no hassle and no fretting. You grab the box and a bottle of syrup and head off to the church for this evening's dinner. Well, here's a better idea: a no fret, fail proof, pancake recipe.

Take 2 cups of flour and add 3 tablespoons of sugar and ½ teaspoon of salt and sift together with 2 teaspoons of baking powder. Heat ¼ cup olive oil in the frying pan while you stir 2¼ cups whole milk (my mother says buttermilk is better—see page 3) into the flour mixture. Separate two eggs, put the yokes into the batter, and whip the whites until stiff. Add the heated oil to the batter, stirring well, and then fold in the egg whites.

Pour ¼ cup onto the hot griddle, allow one side to bubble well, and then flip over. Give it a minute or two on the back side and remove from heat.

You're now ready for the Shrove Tuesday crowds—with a pancake batter that is just as easy as the pre-packaged mix to make, less expensive, better tasting, infinitely expandable (I've used this recipe, times 15, to cook for 100), and fret free.

This last attribute is a key element in the bread of the Jesus circle. Religious types are naturally anxious—always worrying over the state of our soul, the strength of our piety. Daily bread cuts through this angst. It's the first lesson on the road to understanding how Jesus used a shared loaf to bring wholeness. He invited his followers into a tranquil space where their hearts stopped their grasping, scratching search for salvation.

"Can any of you add one hour to life by fretting about it?" So have a pancake and relax your fretful soul. Enjoy the day.

No Fret Pancakes

1. Take 2 cups of flour and add 3 tablespoons of sugar and ½ teaspoon of salt.

2. Sift together with 2 teaspoons of baking powder.

3. Heat ¼ cup olive oil in the frying pan while you stir 2¼ cups whole milk (to make buttermilk take 2% milk, add a touch of lemon juice, and let stand for 5 minutes, or use runny yogurt) into the flour mixture.

4. Separate two eggs, put the yokes into the batter and whip the whites until stiff.

5. Add the heated oil to the batter, stirring well, and then fold in the egg whites.

6. Pour ¼ cup onto the hot griddle, allow one side to bubble well and then flip over.

7. Give it a minute or two on the back side and remove from heat.

Day 1, Ash Wednesday:
Why Worry? A Lesson from Wendy's Cow

Opening Prayer

*I'm still worried. God of eternity, do you know of my uncertainty?
How I hate it when things get out of my control. Tell me what to do.
How do I let go?*

Matthew 6:25

**"That's why I tell you: don't fret about your life—what
you'll eat and drink, or about your body—what you'll
wear. There is more to living than food and clothing,
isn't there?"**

"Don't sweat it!" That's what Wendy would say as the Sunday school
crowd began to spill into the hallway, everyone squealing with delight.
Snack time always produced the same result: a stampede, but Wendy,
the master of any disaster, would quietly restore classroom decorum,
bringing pre-pubescent hormones back into line as the children crunched
their cookies and then quietly returned to the lesson plan. Wendy's
philosophy of keeping calm was magic in the Sunday school, but not new
in her own life...

Back when she was a child growing up in Edmonton, Wendy and her
brother were tormented by a neighbour who would fret over the slightest
intrusion on her space. Take a step off the sidewalk and this older woman
would be at the front window, rapping out her resentment on the plate
glass. Allow an animal to stray onto her manicured lawn and she'd be
standing in the doorstep shaking a finger, scolding both the canine
trespasser and the delinquent child.

At the time of this tale, Wendy's brother worked at the local
slaughterhouse. One day, he came home with a cow. Apparently this
creature had been designated as unfit for the barbecue; it was excess, and

the boss wanted it out of the yard. I don't know what Wendy's brother said to their mother, but you can imagine: "Gee Mom, she won't eat much, and I'll clean out her pen every day. Can we keep her?"

Mother must have been a softie because the cow stayed, but early in the morning the cow began to bray very loudly for breakfast, and the mother (not the sleeping son of course) chased out to the back yard, a fist full of hay in hand, and tried to get the animal to be quiet. Wendy didn't elaborate, but I can imagine her poor mother—dressing gown clutched around her, waving a clump of grass.

Wendy and her brother were eventually enlisted to keep the cow content. Early in the morning they would take it for a walk along the city streets. At first it seemed like a chore, but then an idea took shape: pay back time for the uptight neighbour. As the sun was rising on the tree-lined streets, the siblings walked their cow down to the neighbour's house and allowed the beast to do its business on the lawn. Wendy still smiles as she recounts the way she dealt with the fretting neighbour.

"Don't sweat it." Her philosophy of life. "We'll clear it up."

At first it was just a funny story and then I realized it captures more than Wendy's personal credo. It has a precedent in the Christian gospels. From the Sermon on the Mount found in Matthew, we read: "Don't fret about your life—what you'll eat and drink, or about your body—what you'll wear. There is more to living than food and clothing, isn't there?"

A simple message, as true for today as it was two thousand years ago.

Ash Wednesday has traditionally been a time of super-charged repentance, when the penitent scoured their souls of imperfections. Lent bent spirits were polished with good intentions and the best motives: abstinence, moderation, mortification. But God knows us and loves us in spite of and because of who we are. Stop the fretting and enjoy the ride. That's what our Maker desires most.

A Closing Prayer

> *God, grant me the courage to fret over the big things, the self-confidence to laugh over little ones, and the wisdom to know the difference.*

Day 2:
The Bread that Satisfies

Opening Prayer
> *My life is a scramble for "more." More money, more security, more love. Sometimes it doesn't even matter what the more is. I just need it. God, stop me!*

John 6:35
> **"...Anyone who comes to me will never be hungry again...."**

I heard recently a radio commentator explain that the human species was designed to be an "energy camel." Our physical frame was built to store fat. We began as an animal that fed sporadically. You never knew when the next source of food would come within range and so you had to be able to stockpile carbohydrates. There might have been days or even weeks when our forbearers went without.

Now, the broadcaster's intent was to explore the challenges to diet and physical fitness that our hunter-gatherer origins create for the cosmopolitan lifestyle. The short answer: "Many." You can't take a once-in-a-fortnight animal and feed it three times a day without creating weight issues.

However, I want to stick with the picture of the human creature as a scavenger, a beast with a ravenous appetite. Like our Neolithic ancestors, we are always on the look out for more. You could say we are naturally greedy, but it goes beyond hunger. We are driven by an appetite that's always looking beyond today's meal, watching out for tomorrow's. So "having and holding" is just one side of the equation. We also crave the "getting and going." We're possessed of the spirit of possessing. Put simply, we're an anxious, agitated species.

The table fellowship of Jesus began with clamming this primal hunger. When he broke bread, the restless heart was stilled. The Lord's Supper was an invitation to relax the marauding soul. Somehow the loaf they shared was more than sufficient. It was a miracle meal that truly satisfied.

Day 3:
Late Nights and Shadow Frights

Opening Prayer

> *Time for a confession. How easy it is to pretend that I have it all to-gether—that my life is ordered, my relationships flourishing. But in the night time of my fears, I know it is otherwise. I am plagued by a disquieting nightmare, realizing that all I have is held together loosely. Like a paper kite in a storm, I am contingent and fragile. Where to turn, how to survive? Hold me God, comfort me. Whisper that I am not alone.*

Matthew 6:27

"Can any of you add one hour to life by fretting about it?"

We all do it—worry I mean—and 2:00 a.m. is the perfect time. It begins with a blaring car horn, a child's whimper or a distant siren. No matter the cause, you're suddenly sitting upright, eyes open and alert. Tingling and momentarily frightened, the slightest sound is thunderous. You can hear the creak of the house, the whine of the furnace motor, or the tick of the mantle clock. The flash of fear soon passes as you realize that it was not a life-threatening noise that woke you. You punch the pillow and flop your head back down, groan a few times, and pull up the covers. But sleep does not come.

As you lie there wide-awake, you fret. Your mind starts to cover the familiar territory of missed steps, starting with regular misdemeanours: everything you should have done the day before, the stack of phone messages that are unattended and the list of e-mails languishing in your mailbox. There's the laundry waiting, bills unpaid, appointments missed, money owed. Each infraction is duly noted as you progress to major felonies: the cutting word spoken in haste that ended a relationship and the violent outbreak directed at a loved one. And once you press your recall button, you can go back years and years. So why not dredge up all the misdeeds that are now so old there doesn't seem to be anything you can do to rectify them? People say caffeine keeps you awake, but it doesn't have a patch on rehearsing the litany of our ancient offences.

If you're like me, it will now require several hours of wrestling with your blankets before you fall back to sleep. Usually the sun is just beginning to rise above the horizon.

Are we nocturnal masochists, torturing ourselves by reliving each and every one of our trespasses? Are we naturally anxious beings? Life hangs by a slender thread, and we know it. We're not perfect and we know that too. Our past is clear testimony to our imperfection and when we feel vulnerable, especially at 3:30 a.m., our frailty comes back to haunt us.

Of course, back in our personal histories there is also ample evidence that we have not made enough peace. There are broken fences to be mended and burnt bridges to be built back, and while it is impossible to find a remedy for all our misdeeds, if we pay attention to the recurring nightmares, we may indeed discover who and what is calling out for reconciliation. There may be opportunities to resolve some outstanding debts with a word of apology, a note of explanation, or a confession of affection. It's not easy, but if you want to sleep well, some exploration of the shadows might be in order. Soul work, that's what Lent is for. However, do the exploring in the light of day when your heart is not blindsided by the dark.

Hold it. What if I've got a really big problem or a very old misdemeanour for which there seems nothing I can do? At the risk of sounding clinical, sit with that disquiet for a while—a day in fact. I'll come back to it tomorrow...I do have a solution in mind, but first we must reacquaint ourselves with our finitude before freedom is possible.

If you're awake and can't sleep, why not sing? Here are a few evening hymn suggestions from *Voices United*: "Day is Done" (VU #433), "The Day You Gave" (VU #437), "Unto the Hills" (VU #842).

Day 4:
The Morning After the Night Before

Opening Prayer

Dear God, wake me up to who you are. Open my eyes to see you, not the cheap show or the pious platitudes. Give me strength to see you as you are: bread for the journey, not too much, not too little. Just enough.

Matthew 6:31–32

"So don't fret. Don't say, 'What am I going to eat?' or 'What am I going to drink?' or 'What am I going to wear?' These are all things the 'pagans' seek. After all, your heavenly Father is aware you need them."

You're still awake? Yesterday, I left you riding the twilight roller coaster of regret and recrimination and I promised a cure—an emotional decongestant that would unclog stopped-up guilt glands and relax any restless soul.

Wait. Before I offer this miraculous elixir for the worry-worn soul, let's be clear about one thing. All religions are united in their desire to keep their faithful, faithful. They want customers who will come back again and again. They're not in the business of turning disciples into self-taught, self-directed beings. Consequently, priests and pastors consciously or unconsciously guard their soul food under lock and key— passing it out in measured portions. So I'm speaking out of school when I sell you a "medicine" for your nocturnal neuroses without first requiring that you sign on the dotted line for a specific religious commitment.

All right, I am poking a little fun at my own profession, but it's good to remember that God hates any religion that places itself between the Eternal Lover and the beloved. Pious leaders who put a price on God's goodness often block the way to heaven. As soon as spiritual truths become "secrets," reserved only for the deserving few, then we are lost.

Hence, if I look like I am dispensing a prescription-only antibiotic as if it was an over-the-counter drug...well, I am. The solution to your middle of the night blues is...*The morning sunrise!*

The old adage remains true—things do look better in the morning. The fresh dawn air has a miraculous healing power—wiping away our worries. Call it instinctive or intuitive, the human soul registers a lift at sunrise because we experience again the deep truth that in every morning we are given another chance. The minutes and hours ahead of us are an opportunity to make things right.

In a deeper sense, we also sense a continuing and constant promise in the new day. Our Creator declares with brilliant rays that the night does not last forever. There is an order to creation—out of darkness comes light. Out of death comes new life. Out of our great sorrow comes an equal portion of rejoicing.

People ask me about the meaning of Easter. I can think of no more satisfying response than a sunrise. In this festival we extol a God who is immanent. Not detached or ethereal, the God of scripture is close, as real as a sunrise. Every dawn declares that we are not alone, that forgiveness is tangible and that we have been given a new chance to live out the promise of our birth. And above all else, the dawn is a pure gift. It's freely given. You can't achieve it. You don't win it or earn it. It is a testament to an All Giving Maker.

The monstrous doubts of the night remain solid and immoveable until I look to the dawn and see them vanish. Then I realize how fortunate I am. God makes the sun to rise each day, no judgment, no pre-condition, just an invitation to celebrate.

This could descend into platitudes and it is for that reason that we are never allowed to fritter away our suffering as if it did not exist or was easily overcome. The midnight roller coaster is real. Nevertheless—and this is the big nevertheless of the Bible—your doubts and worries do not have the last word—neither on you nor on your worth.

The First Sunday in Lent:
A Sabbatical Break, Two Reasons to Rest

Opening Prayer

> *Sometimes I try too hard to finish my own story, control the dialogue, tie up the loose ends, and finish the plot. God, keep me open, allowing your mystery to unfold of its own accord.*

Exodus 20:8-11

> **Remember the Sabbath day and keep it holy. For six days you shall labour and do all your work, but the seventh day is a Sabbath for Yahweh your God….For in six days Yahweh made the heavens and the earth and sea and all that these contain, but on the seventh day he rested.**

The Ten Commandments appear twice in scripture, once in Deuteronomy and once in Exodus. No big deal. I always say that a good sermon deserves to be preached more than once. With regard to The Ten Commandments, a close reading of the two versions will indicate that while the essentials are exactly the same, there are a few subtle differences.

Take the injunction to keep the Sabbath. The actual regulation is consistent from one book to the next. "Thou shalt keep the Sabbath day…." But the motivation for this practice changes. In Deuteronomy it's a question of justice. If you were slaves in Egypt and were given your freedom, you also should extend that privilege to all that you have—your household and domestic animals. Even the earth itself should rest. Take a break because it is God's wish that our lives be ruled by distributive justice. In contrast, the Exodus version is moved by sanctification. The author reflects on how our God created the earth in six days and on the seventh rested. We, who worship this God, should reflect this divine repose by resting ourselves. A sabbatical is an act of devotion.

In this guide I am going to invite you to take a regular sabbatical break—no bread making, no heavy work. Let this first time out be motivated by Exodus thinking when your repose is a gift of eternity within time. Now is all that you have. Don't look back to the six previous days of labour. Don't fret over the coming week's work. Breathe deeply and look closely at those in your circle. See them as the blessing they are. Remember again that you also are a gift of a loving Creator.

Some "thou shalt's" are heavy-handed and harsh. This one is gentle and inviting. Amen!

Day 5:
Is Fasting Out of Fashion?

Opening Prayer

> *God of the human way, hold me up when I falter over pious words and grow weary of my pompous preening. Lift me when I stumble over my own arrogance. Bring me back to your world, to its richness and bounty.*

Matthew 6:16-18a

> **"When you fast, don't make a spectacle of your remorse as the pretenders do. As you know, they make their faces unrecognizable so they may be publicly recognized. I swear to you they have been paid in full. When you fast, comb your hair and wash your face, so your fasting my go unrecognized...."**

For the past nine years I have been producing a weekly spirituality column. People ask: "After that length of time, even God grows thin. What keeps you going?" My answer is: "I nibble." For instance, as I type this evening I have a plate of crackers lathered in cheese spread at my right hand. Is it the actual chewing or the contented afterglow of a full stomach? I don't know, but food helps me concentrate on the Holy.

It is therefore strange that during this period of Lent, Christian penitents go without nourishment on purpose. No bread, daily or otherwise. It's not a new fad. Almost as soon as the human spirit conceived of an "almighty god," the notion of depriving oneself of eating arose. But in an over-indulgent, over-weight world fasting seems like anathema, a laughable relic carried over from pre-enlightenment superstition. However, before we scoff too loudly, let us examine the logic of self-denial carefully. There are three classic arguments for the importance and relevance of fasting.

First, it has been suggested by many saints and scholars that the most serious obstacle separating God and humanity is our pretence. We believe that we are more important than we actually are, that we have more skill in manipulating and controlling our destiny than is reasonable, and that we can attain levels of virtue that are impossible.

Pride. There is nothing intrinsically wrong with being proud of our achievements, but when we take pride in things that we have not done or could never hope to accomplish, then we are living an illusory life. Fasting, because it weakens the body, tends to undermine this natural process of pretence. It brings us down from our ivory towers and reminds us that we are a frail, often faulted species. I can't imagine that God enjoys our hunger or is actually honoured by children who are suffering self-inflicted denial, but fasting might help us to be real, to accept our true state as created beings that are dependent on the love of our Maker.

Second, because it reminds us of our basic state as creatures, fasting opens us to the possibility of trust. When our belly is full, it is easy to stand alone. If there is no community, then trust dies and along with it, faith and hope fade. Our hunger helps us to understand how much we need others for support—physical and spiritual aid. If, through fasting, we can learn to trust one another more, perhaps we will also find the strength to trust our God more thoroughly as well.

Finally, fasting is ironically the pause that refreshes. Stress, family dynamics, and, yes, writing deadlines cause me to eat more. It's a natural response, and fasting breaks that behaviour in a way that allows the believer a moment of clarity in which to sort out their priorities.

All too often you'll hear about "mortifying the flesh." It's a crude and misguided notion that the physical world is evil and less important than the spiritual realm. So we punish our bodies for their sinfulness in order to rise up to rewards of a heavenly existence. This is nonsense! God created the earth and loves it—our bodies included. So rather than speak of fasting as penitence, why not think of it as a "time out."

Three good reasons to fast, but remember, fasting is one of the most demanding of religious disciplines and it's not intended to be a perpetual practice. Those who suffer from eating disorders may wisely pass. In truth, let us fast sparingly since, in the end, God wants us to rejoice in the richness of this planet—cheese spread and all.

Day 6:
First You Fall In

Opening Prayer
> *God, keep my hands still. Lift my eyes to the skies—help me to be
> still and know that you are my Maker. You made me in your image,
> and your hand is always close—to protect and feed. Amen.*

Matthew 6:26
> **"Take a look at the birds of the sky: they don't plant or
> harvest or gather into barns. Yet your heavenly Father
> feeds them. You're worth more than they, aren't you?"**

"First, you fall in love." Sound familiar? Didn't you utter that phrase once
or twice in your job as the mentor and guide to a hopelessly intimidated
adolescent? A Cinderella-like bedtime story recounted by anxious parents
to both panicky and know-it-all offspring. It makes sense. Who wouldn't
begin explaining about the birds and bees by pointing to the most powerful
of emotions—love? But what if those five words were the opening sentence
of the Koran, the Bible or Bhagavid-Gita. Would they still make sense?

When Westerners think about sacred writings, they might imagine
a Charlton Heston-like deity, one who commands the waves of the sea
and the ways of men with equal dispassion. The good book is about rules
and commandments, "Thou Shalts" and "Thou Shalt Nots." At a stretch
it could be a cultic tome of deep wisdom, a place where the mysterious
"goddess of insight" and creativity pokes her head through the fog we
call rationality, and to theologians, the scriptures are a fount of doctrinal
knowledge, the source of all questions, and the basis for all answers, if
only we know where to look. But love? Surely not! You don't believe it
can be that easy?

Imagine that you're looking around for solace for your soul and so
you enter the shadowed sanctity of a place of worship. Finding the leader,
you ask where to begin. What will you hear? Ah...

The well-schooled in religious matters will probably argue that the pilgrimage into the heart of God, the journey directed by the sacred books—mind you—is a pathway of trusting and faith. And before many kind words are spoken, even before you sit or kneel down, you'll start to hear about principles that govern God and his disciples, laws that rule the universe and her children: how you must begin to think, what you must do, how you must see or in some cases not see your neighbours. Of course, it's not always recited in imperatives. Sometimes, hopefully more often than not, the pitch is delivered with a kind gesture or welcoming bowl of soup. But under the heavy hand of spiritual patronage or even behind the light touch of compassionate guidance, there is an unwritten assumption that dogma counts. After all, that's what "orthodoxy" means.

But the noblest of mental equations can't prove God's existence. Healthy religion starts with love. First you fall in love. All the creeds and confessions matter not a wit, if first you do not know yourself as a loveable and loving child of earth—a message embedded in Matthew's Sermon on the Mount: "Take a look at the birds of the sky: they don't plant or harvest or gather into barns. Yet your heavenly Father feeds them. You're worth more than they, aren't you?"

The God, revealed in Jesus, loves you. And I don't mean in some pious other worldly sense. Flesh and blood—we are made from the earth. We fall in love with those close to us, the ones we can touch and who touch us. Our proximity to our heavenly God—you pick the name—is governed by how much we love those down here on earth.

I am constantly struck by how many pop songs talk about love, parade its perfection, and lament its loss. While some of this ranting can be explained as the sentimentality of an empty culture, much of this yearning for love is indeed the desire to know unconditional acceptance—one that is not frightened off by tears and betrayal—in a word, God. Celine Dion's song is a fine example: *"I'll be waiting for you, here inside my heart. I'm the one who wants to love you more. Can't you see I can give you everything you need? Let me be the one to love you more."*

God couldn't say it better if She tried. Waiting there in your heart is the One who whispers, "First you fall in love."

Day 7:
The True North Strong and Easter

Opening Prayer
> *Thank you, God—all is not lost, the winter has not won. Spring ushers in your promises of new life. Amen and Hallejuah!*

Mark 16:5–6
> **And when they went into the tomb, they saw a young man sitting on the right, wearing a white robe, and they grew apprehensive. He says to them, "Don't be alarmed! You are looking for Jesus the Nazarene who was crucified. He was raised, he is not here!"**

A classic melody in Quebec begins with a startling vision: "*Mon pays ce n'est pas un pays, c'est l'hiver.*" Roughly translated: "My country is not a country, it's winter." You don't have to speak French to agree, but I would alter it slightly to suit the Christian high season. What if we sang, "My country is not a country, it's Easter"?

Think of Easter as more than a Christian festival commemorating the resurrection of Jesus of Nazareth. It can also be understood as a moment when disciples of Christ rejoice in the miracle of new life. In that sense it could be a holy day for secularist and believer alike. Buddhists, Muslims, Jews, Jains or Hindus would shout with gladness: "Amen. Death is not the final word. There is always a sunrise that follows the night." But if Easter is a tale of re-birth, why would I consider Canada to be a particularly appropriate embodiment of the Paschal message?

First, there is no better example than Canada of the vibrancy of life and irrepressible force of revitalization that is built right into Mother Nature herself. Depending on where you live in this true north, strong and frozen, you have between three and six months of the deep chill, an annual event where the land is freeze-dried into a monolithic block of lost hope. The lawns turn brown and are then blanketed in successive layers of white. Trees lose their greenery and look like dead skeletons. Roads become ice rinks, and our famous lakes and streams pull up the covers for a long winter's nap. There's nothing alive in the northern winter landscape, and anyone coming from another planet would move on to more fertile territory.

So when the thermometer drops, Canadians bury their noses in scarves and muffs and dash for shelter. We shovel our walks with listless despair and discuss endlessly the plagues of winter weather. Monday morning commuters shovel out their vehicles with the resignation of a chain gang—and with about as much enthusiasm. Friday evening coffee clubs debate the merits of chains over studs on tires, and in a perverse self-flagellating manner, everyone boasts about the size of the snow banks in their hometown—the higher the mound the more virtuous the inhabitants.

And yet out of this block of ice comes a people of surprising resilience. Just when you think we're beyond redemption, the people emerge and sprout wings. Tulips push through the permafrost, dreams are dusted off, the robins return, and we know we will live another season. I offer a Canadian spring as a metaphor for Easter because in this arctic climate we know, perhaps more clearly than those people of southern climes, that winter is a killer. The fact that we can make it to another spring is truly a miracle.

Canadians are not cheap believers; we do not give easy credence to ideas, concepts or even our own gods. Perhaps that is our charm, and in the last analysis, a saving grace when it comes to Easter. Not prone to extravagance or exaggeration, our celebrations of new life have a genuine quality. We know the darkness of our fears all too well and therefore have special reverence for dawn's first light.

Hallelujah!

The Second Ingredient of Daily Bread Discipleship

Bread is Bread

Day 8:
Bread is Bread

Opening Prayer
> *God of wheat and wine. Bring me down from my high-flying prayers to find you in bread and wine. Sustenance for the body, delight for the soul.*

Mark 6:41-42
> **And he took the five loaves and two fishes....**
> **Everybody had more than enough to eat.**

Faith suffers when people try too hard. For instance, it has been my experience that when we open the sacred scripture, we treat it like a mysterious icon that contains hidden meanings. Putting on kid gloves, we ignore the superficial meanings, hunting for the treasure we presume is buried beneath the adjectives and adverbs. We turn each parable upside down, exploring what is written underneath, finding allegorical meanings that predict everything from the second coming of the messiah to tomorrow's weather.

While I would be first in line to suggest that the Bible needs to be read carefully, there are times when we lose the point if we try to be too sophisticated. Take the Lord's Supper for example. Two thousand years of devotion and exegesis have overlaid that table fellowship with such ornate linens—rich ritual and priestly prerogatives—that we can hardly make out the meal that lies at its heart. Yet we have ample evidence that first and foremost when people gathered around Jesus, there was food—real food for hungry bodies.

The stories of the feeding of the multitude are key to understanding how Jesus used bread to spread the message of the coming reign of God. Don't look to heaven. The central point is contained in a shared loaf. According to Mark, when the preaching is completed, the disciples are worried—not because the people are shouting for more spiritual direction. They are hungry, literally. They need a meal. And their master gives them bread. When people gathered in Jesus' company there was abundance—lots of bread.

In this Lenten time, we focus on a second ingredient in Christian discipleship: disciples of Christ share bread as bread. The abundance of bread, as sustenance for the body, was and is a cornerstone of our ministry.

So give a boost to your faith—eat bread—share a slice with a friend. It's a start.

If you're looking for some new ways to shape bread, most of the days within this section are accompanied by a bread recipe.

Day 9:
The Bread of Heaven

Opening Prayer

> *God of busybodies and frightened souls, slow me down and blunt my fears. I'm rushing about because I don't trust that you will provide. It's a dog-eat-dog world out there and I'm…Okay, I'm listening… You say you'll send me bread from heaven—a slice, that's all. Just my share? You've got to be kidding!*

Matthew 6:11
> **Give us this day our daily bread.**

Bread is more than carbohydrates and fibre. It's soul food. Jesus knew that when he coined the phrase, "Give us this day our daily bread." The effort we expend in finding and shaping the nourishment we need for the day is time not spent killing our human spirit. When you're up to your elbows in bread dough, you can't strike out at a neighbour—not easily. And with that sticky paste covering your fingers, how can you grasp for more useless toys or trinkets? Let's make some bread and think about how it fosters heart-filled peace and contentment.

> *Take 2 level tablespoons of dry yeast, a teaspoon of sugar, and ½ cup of warm water, and mix it together. Let it stand for 10 minutes while you put 8 cups of white flour, ⅓ a cup each of sugar and olive oil, and a tablespoon of salt in a bowl. Mix in 2 cups of warm water. (2 eggs are optional.)*

Okay, you'll probably have a minute to wait for the yeast, so now you can do what every baker does: think about who will eat your bread, beginning with yourself. In your mind, you can taste the fresh, soft dough, smothered in butter and jam and you ask yourself if there is any better meal on earth. And then you relish the smiles that homemade loaves always bring to your circle. The rich fragrance of baking bread is an antidote to all ills.

Right, now we stir the yeast into the flour mixture and start kneading. For folks who don't like television exercise shows, kneading bread is a good home-grown workout. Ten minutes on the flour board and your bread dough will get the heart rate up, improve upper body strength, and improve endurance. I use the palms of my hands pushing and folding the dough in any way that suits my fancy. You can use your fingers and squeeze it, roll it with forearms, or turn it into a football and play catch. Some folk see this stage of bread making as a chance to take out pent up aggression on the unsuspecting (and forgiving) dough — so flail away. There's no rule here, just work the dough until the natural gluten transforms the mass of flour into an elastic ball. If your dough is still stiff, add a tad more water.[2] A touch more flour if it's still sticking to your hands. Kneading will take 10 to 15 minutes, so you might want to take a break midway through.

While you catch your breath, think on this simple fact. Hand kneading your bread, while it takes longer than a machine, is an excellent restraint on impulse shopping. When we're busy punching and pounding it, we don't have time to hoard more than our share.

Back to the kneading—just a few more minutes.

When Jesus called this "our daily bread" he was inviting his followers to recall that the chief quality of the daily bread of the wilderness, manna, was "enough." The people of the desert couldn't take an excess of this bread of heaven or squirrel some away for a rainy day. So Jesus is saying, in this central prayer: "Give us enough."

Your bread is ready to rise. Roll it into a ball and plop it into a greased bread bowl. Cover with a damp cloth. Two hours later, tip it onto a floured board, shape 3 loaves, and place them in regular size, buttered bread pans. After 2 more hours, bake at 325° for ³/₄ hour.

Presto, a loaf for you, one for your intimates, and one to give away. This simple recipe can be altered to make bagels, pizza dough, and raisin bread—but for now, cut off a few large slices, get out the honey, and call

---

2. Watch the additional water—you will be surprised how little will make a difference. Start with a touch and work the dough before adding more.

a friend. Listen for the lift in their voice when you invite them to your feast. "Fresh bread? I'll be right over." Soul food indeed!

Daily Bread
(from the above devotional)

1. Take 2 level tablespoons of dry yeast, a teaspoon of sugar, and ½ cup of warm water, and mix it together. Let it stand for 10 minutes.

2. Put 8 cups of white flour, ⅓ a cup each of sugar and olive oil, 1 tablespoon of salt in a bowl. Mix in 2 cups of warm water. (2 eggs are optional.)

3. Once yeast is foamy, stir it into the flour mixture and start kneading.

4. Knead for 10 to 15 minutes. (If your dough is still stiff, add a tad more water; a touch more flour if it's still sticking to your hands.)

5. Roll it into a ball and plop it into a greased bread bowl. Then cover with a damp cloth.

6. Two hours later, tip it out onto a floured board, shape 3 loaves, and place them in regular size, buttered bread pans.

7. Allow 2–2½ hours more to rise and bake them at 325°F for ¾ hour. (Temperature from 325°-375°F, depending on your oven.)

Day 10:
Shaping Our Loaves from the Bread of Heaven

Opening Prayer

> *God of the desert—save me from my best intentions. The brave dreams I have for tomorrow confound me and take me away from my center. Guide my hands to shape today's bread according to your design.*

Deuteronomy 30:19

> **I call heaven and earth to witness against you today that I have set before you life and death, blessings and curses. Choose life so that you and your descendants may live….**

Do I have a tendency to leave folks in their own lurch, just at the key point in a learning exercise? Take yesterday. I said, "Shape three loaves and place them in regular size, buttered bread pans." To the experienced hand on the breadboard this is the simple part. But to the novice, this rolling and pinching looks like magic. So let me explain. When you've done with the kneading and the dough has risen once, we arrive at the loaf-shaping step. There are three things to remember:

First, making a pleasing loaf is an art form. Once your dough has doubled in size, it's a lump of clay looking for a potter, and that's you! And you can relax, there are no mistakes. If you get the dough into a pan, no matter how misshaped it might look, it will bake up into a tasty delight. Second, it's best to have the necessary tools at hand, before you start. You'll need to get the margarine out of the fridge, a flour shaker if you have one, the loaf pans, a dry, sharp knife, and clean hands. Third, if bread making were like gardening, this stage is that rewarding time when we water, weed, and admire the new growth that has sprung from our fingers. So an audience at this stage is not a bad thing—let the whole family admire your handiwork.

Okay, we have to butter the pans. Make sure that they are thoroughly dry—moisture will cause the dough to stick to the pan. You don't want a thick layer of butter, just a light smearing will do. Pay special attention to the corners and bottom—that's where the dough loves to hold out when you tip over the cooked loaf.

While you're greasing up the pans, let's think about the watershed in the story of God's people in this reading from Deuteronomy. Moses and his followers are pictured on the mountaintop overlooking the Promised Land. Can you feel the breeze in your hair as they survey their fondest dream coming into view? But the prophet stops them on the brink of their fantasy and calls them to account: **"I call heaven and earth to witness against you today that I have set before you life and death, blessings and curses."** For Moses life was the desert, death was the land flowing with milk and honey. In the barren land people trusted their Maker to send bread from heaven. In the settled lands they will rely on the king's bread. Something deadly happens when the people begin to shape their own loaves, buying and selling them, rather than waiting upon their God to provide.

Back to the breadboard! Dust it lightly with flour—not too much. Cut the dough into six equal pieces and separate each on the floured surface. Take one portion with both hands, roll it into a ball, and then pull back on edges to break out a clean surface on one side. Place the ball, clean surface up, onto a dry surface. Now, using the edge of your hands, not the palms, roll the dough in a clockwise motion. Your little finger and the edge of your hand will be pushing the bottom edges of your dough ball in toward the center as you roll the dough. You're not pressing on the top of the dough at all. You may need all five other portions of dough to perfect this technique, but in the end, you'll have a nice tight loaf with all the wrinkles on the bottom. Place two side by side into each of your three pans (creases down): bum-bread. The two balls provide better surface tension, and the dough will rise higher than a single loaf can.

Think of Moses. He knew people would soon start to use their bread to make distinctions. Leaving behind the equitable life of daily bread, they would start to accumulate wealth—speculating on and exploiting each other's hunger. They would trust their own designs and forget the basic shape of heaven-sent bread. **"Choose life so that you and your descendants may live…."** Choose the life that takes each day as a gift of God—that knows from whom and to whom we come.

Our life is like the dough. We are given the great gift of shaping it according to our own designs or the designs provided by our Creator: life or death. **"Choose life!"** But don't sweat it. Rejoice. If we calm our unsettled hearts, and turn them to God's purposes and help, there are no mistakes.

Daily Bread
(Now you know about shaping, you can try the recipe again.)

1. Take 2 level tablespoons of dry yeast, a teaspoon of sugar, and ½ cup of warm water, and mix it together. Let it stand for 10 minutes.

2. Put 8 cups of white flour, ⅓ a cup each of sugar and olive oil, 1 tablespoon of salt in a bowl. Mix in 2 cups of warm water. (2 eggs are optional.)

3. Once yeast is foamy, stir it into the flour mixture and start kneading.

4. Knead for 10 to 15 minutes. (If your dough is still stiff, add a tad more water; a touch more flour if it's still sticking to your hands.)

5. Roll it into a ball and plop it into a greased bread bowl. Then cover with a damp cloth.

6. Two hours later, tip it out onto a floured board, shape 3 loaves, and place them in regular size, buttered bread pans.

7. Allow 2-2½ hours more to rise and bake them at 325°F for ¾ hour. (Temperature from 325°–375°F, depending on your oven.)

The Second Sunday in Lent:
A Sabbatical Summary

Opening Prayer
> *Give me this day my daily bread—no more, no less. Just enough!*

Deuteronomy 5:12-15
> **Observe the Sabbath day and keep it holy as Yahweh your God has commanded you. Labor for six days, doing all your work, but the seventh day is a Sabbath for Yahweh your God....Remember you were once a slave in Egypt and that Yahweh your God brought you out of there with mighty hand and outstretched arm: this is why Yahweh your God has commanded you keep the Sabbath day.**

The author of Deuteronomy supplemented the fifth commandment with an explanation that God had brought the people out of slavery. The reason for the day off was based on reciprocity. Once the sons and daughters of Abraham had been worked mercilessly—slaves without right or relief. Then Yahweh had brought them out with a mighty arm. Now that they enjoy liberty, they are bound to extend this grace to others.

There are times when I wish I could re-write scripture passages—this one for sure. The problem is that the motivating principle of justice comes in the wrong place. Most people hear the bold commandment loud and clear, but don't bother with the fine print. Who knows why we take a holiday every seven days? We do it because we were told to do it. God demands obedience. Consequently, the institution of a Sabbath break has no depth. It becomes a religious duty. (One that we will ignore as soon as economics demand it.) Action based on duty soon turns to resentment or self-righteousness.

A better start is to reverse the order. Grace first, then comes the human response. The gift is given—without condition or prerequisite.

Liberation is extended to the chosen ones. In the best of circumstances, those who have been gifted quite genuinely want to reciprocate—to give freedom to others. That's the logic of a Sabbath—you have been blessed with a break. Follow the natural pathway of your heart and extend the blessing to all around you.

Jesus was depending on this innate response of generosity when he introduced the idea of daily bread into his disciples' prayer life. He wasn't expecting people to hoard their day's stash. Rather, once you've been freely given your slice of today's loaf, you'll want to share your abundance with others. Justice doesn't need a catchy slogan or spin doctor. Make it happen once, and faithful people pass it on.

Day 11:
The Perfect Sandwich Pocket

Opening Prayer
> *God of the delights, open my heart to surprise.*

Mark 6:41-42
> **And he took the five loaves and two fishes, looked up to the sky, gave a blessing, and broke the bread apart, and started giving it to his disciples to pass around to them....**

There's no greater threat to Christian discipleship than self-assured faith. Think about that while we make some more bread...

First, proof your yeast— ¹⁄₂ cup warm water, 1 teaspoon sugar, and 2 tablespoons of yeast sprinkled over the top. Let it stand. Mix together 8 cups of flour, ¹⁄₂ cup oil, 2¹⁄₂ cups warm water, ¹⁄₄ cup sugar, 3 eggs, 1 tablespoon salt, and ¹⁄₂ cup wheat germ.

Any devout church-goer is the inheritor of two thousand years of instruction and doctrine. A well-informed believer has heard the "old, old story" told so often that they already know every twist and turn in the journey. There are no surprises left. There's no tension of anticipation, no thrill of expectation, and faith is seriously crippled when surprise is taken out of its heart. If you know the ending to all the healing stories and you can see the dark cross of Golgotha only in the bright light of an Easter resurrection, what's the point? Alas, we have been trained well to read scripture backwards from the triumph of the empty tomb, so that the gospel's subversive element is buried in our stampede to the Jerusalem. The edge of parables has been dulled, and the liberating messages behind the miracles are lost to sight. Jesus, rather than being a Palestinian peasant with an attitude, has become the quintessential Victorian gentleman reclining on the cross. So we mold him with too much ease into the conclusion to every spiritual or ethical dilemma.

There was once a minister who in telling the children's story was "plagued" with the problem of facing the kids each week; so his stories were usually thinly veiled moralisms that boiled down to "Jesus loves me, this I know since the Bible tells me so." On this particular Sunday, he began with a little riddle: "Boys and girls, what's brown and fuzzy, hops across your lawn and chews nuts, and has a long bushy tail?" Up goes a hand in the back. "Ooo…," squeals a youngster. The pastor grins. Ah… someone to save his bacon. "Okay Michelle, what's the answer?" The bright girl responds, "Well, it sounds like a squirrel, but I'll bet it's Jesus."

Is that our faith? The tasteless conventional "beliefulness" that expects nothing new and tricks itself into seeing every furry animal in the Bible as Jesus in disguise.

Once the yeast is frothy, you can mix it with the flour and knead well—15 minutes minimum. You want a smooth and elastic dough.

Our reading of scripture is particularly prone to this predictability. Turn over any leaf in the New Testament and there is Jesus staring back. Our fixation on Christ has meant that every Bible story is heard as either a foreshadowing or affirmation of his Lordship. There are times when we have to get Jesus out of the picture in order to hear what the gospels are proclaiming.

A quick example of this is the feeding of the five thousand. Right up there with walking on water and changing water into wine, it is the kind of biblical legend that sends my mind into hibernation. Nothing new, so I go to sleep. The crowds follow their miracle worker into the wilderness and such is his appeal that they wait throughout the long, hot day, hanging on every word. When the time for dinner comes, the throng is still there, and the disciples start to worry. How will they feed such a huge company? Jesus stills their hand-wringing and has the people sit. Taking the one-person box-lunch the disciples have found, Jesus blesses the bread and some fish and then gives it out to the expectant mob.

Are you excited? Waiting on the cusp of curiosity? No. We know the punch line. Jesus turns the few small loaves into a feast for the whole throng. There's enough for all and even a great surplus left over. And here's where our programmed faith takes over. We think the tale is only about the potency of Jesus.

Roll your dough into a greased bowl, cover with a damp tea towel, and let rise for 2 hours.

If we get the "triumph Jesus" out of the way, we will see there is also a deeper message. The early Christian community circle saw the multiplication of bread in the wilderness as a message of justice. When bread passes through Jesus' hand there is enough for all. No one starves in the company of Christ. Reflecting the early Christian practice of sharing all they had, this desert feast is assurance that God creates bread for the company. All are fed. No one is turned away. A miracle!

Now for the fun. Let's turn up the heat: set your oven at 500°. Once the dough has doubled in size, roll it out onto a floured surface and divide into 24 equal size pieces. Shape each into a ball and let stand for 10 minutes. Using a rolling pin, flatten each ball into a 6-inch circle. Place each one on a baking dish sprinkled with cornmeal. Put the dish onto the bottom rack of the hot oven—leave it for 4 minutes and then shift it to the top rack for another 4 minutes. (This way you can continue to rotate pitas into the oven.) After the 8 minutes, you will have a nicely browned miracle—a rounded pita bun, doughy and tender—the perfect sandwich pocket. Let cool on the counter before eating.

Like the miracle of feeding the multitudes, making pitas looks like magic. Have the kids near at hand to witness God's goodness. (And to taste it!) The Jesus bread, the daily variety, was always abundant, reflecting the mystery and magic of manna. In his company the lost are found, the outcast are taken in, and the starving are fed.

Pita Bread

1. Proof your yeast—½ cup warm water, 1 teaspoon sugar and 2 tablespoons of yeast sprinkled over top. Let stand 10 minutes.

2. Mix together 8 cups of flour, ½ cup oil, 2½ cups warm water, ¼ cup sugar, 3 eggs, 1 tablespoon salt, and ½ cup wheat germ.

3. Once the yeast is frothy, mix it with the flour and knead well— 15 minutes minimum. You want a smooth and elastic dough. Put the dough into a greased bowl, cover with a damp tea towel, and let stand 2 hours.

4. Pre-heat oven at 500°F.

5. Once the dough has doubled in size, roll it out onto a floured surface and divide into 24 equal size pieces. Shape each into a ball and let stand for 10 minutes.

6. Using a rolling pin, flatten each ball into a 6-inch circle.

7. Place each one on a baking dish sprinkled with cornmeal. Put the dish onto the bottom rack of the hot oven—leave it for 4 minutes and then shift it to the top rack for another 4 minutes. (This way you can continue to rotate pitas into the oven.)

8. After the 8 minutes you will have a nicely browned miracle—a rounded pita bun, doughy and tender—the perfect sandwich pocket. Let cool on the counter before eating.

Fill with falafel, cheese, or your favourite sandwich mix.

Day 12:
Bread for the Journey

Opening Prayer

> *God, ruler of light and shadow, when I am hungry, feed me, when I am lost, bring me home, and when I am cowering, stand by me 'til I rise up.*

Matthew 6:34

> **"So don't fret about tomorrow. Let tomorrow fret about itself. The troubles that the day brings are enough."**

I used to understand what was happening under the hood of my car. Cylinders and spark plugs churned together in a harmony of internal combustion. A gas line feeding the carburettor, powering the generator made the melody complete. Now when I pop the lid, I have trouble even recognizing the engine. Tubes and computers have taken over from belts and points.

You may feel that way about bread. It's a mystery that only bakers understand. In like fashion, there are many folk who feel that same twinge of alienation when the word "spirituality" is raised. Their eyes glaze over as they assume that it involves a deep, hidden science of the soul that only the most sophisticated could understand or manipulate. Those of us who are diligent might pick up a self-help manual or two, but often the very concept of leading a spirit-filled life alludes us. We assume we don't know the secret incantations that bring inner enlightenment.

Here's a recipe that takes away the mystery of flat bread: Armenian spice sheets. Proof 1 tablespoon of yeast in a cup of warm water with 1 teaspoon of sugar. Melt ½ cup butter at the same time and put it in the freezer to cool. When yeast is frothy, add the butter to the yeast and mix in 2 cups of white flour. Stir it around until it's well mixed and then add another cup of flour, 1 teaspoon of salt to make a stiff dough. Now knead it for 10 minutes.

A journalist once approached an indisputable Canadian saint, Jean Vanier, and asked him about his spirituality. After all, a man who has written so much on the topic should be well versed in the labyrinth of the human heart. So the interviewer began with a straightforward question: "What are the important aspects that feed your soul?"

Now, you'd imagine that Jean would respond with a description of his prayer life, the endless hours on his knees. Perhaps he would reveal the secrets of the universe that were revealed to him in his moments of ecstatic possession by the Holy Spirit. But Vanier began on a very human level. He said that his soul was fed by the chef of their community who made the most excellent French sauces.

Now that you've finished the kneading you can now let your bread stand for 2 hours.

Before the journalist had time to draw breath in protest, Vanier went on to suggest that his spiritual life was also nourished by the community because they laughed a great deal. Finally, Vanier argued that his soul found its best food by looking into the eyes of those with whom he lived. We see the spirit in each other. Three very mundane activities were the wellspring that filled this man's inner needs. You might say that Vanier's spiritual life could be summarized as "shared bread."

Once the bread dough has doubled, divide it into 4 balls. Preheat the oven to 350°, and then using a rolling pin make each ball into a very thin oval—14 to 20 inches wide. Place on an ungreased cookie sheet, sprinkle with spices (herbs of Provence or Italian seasoning or poppy and sesame seeds; chile or paprika will give it a slightly hotter taste; grated cheese would be a nice touch). Press these spices into the thin dough, pop the sheet into the oven, and cook for 15 to 20 minutes. The bread will get quite brown—that's the way it should be.

A simple definition of spirituality: meeting God in the French sauce, in the laughter of our community or in a crisp flat bread (perfect to dip in the sauce or hummus or antipasto).

In contrast to the trends of car maintenance, it is time for the religious elite to come out from behind our sanctimonious enclosures and admit that the spiritual path is an open shop. You don't need to be an expert. Everyone can, indeed must, become their soul's mechanic.

Armenian Flat Bread

1. Proof 1 tablespoon of yeast in cup of warm water with 1 teaspoon sugar.

2. Melt ½ cup butter and put in freezer to cool.

3. When yeast is frothy, add melted butter and mix in 2 cups white flour.

4. Stir until well mixed and add another cup of flour, 1 teaspoon salt to make stiff dough.

5. Knead for 10 minutes. Let stand for 2 hours.

6. When dough has doubled in size, divide into 4 balls.

7. Preheat oven to 350°F.

8. Using a rolling pin, make each ball into a very thin oval (14-20 inches wide).

9. Place on ungreased cookie sheet and sprinkle with spices and/or cheese. Press spices/cheese into the dough.

10. Cook for 15-20 minutes. The bread should be quite brown.

Day 13:
No Hunger

Opening Prayer

God of the desert, open my heart to see you in the wilderness times of my life—maybe then I will taste again the bread you send from heaven and learn to trust you more deeply.

John 6:35

Jesus explained to them, "I am the bread of life. Anyone who comes to me will never be hungry again, and anyone who believes in me will never again be thirsty."

There are a number of obstacles to hearing the good news that Jesus gives bread that sustains us. For instance, very few North Americans have suffered through a famine. Consequently, we don't have first-hand experience of the extended hunger that was common among the followers of Jesus. Hearing the story of the feeding of the multitudes, the first audience of the gospel would marvel at the overflowing abundance—baskets brimming with bread and fish. Modern minds are fixated on the magic of multiplication. The evangelists told the tale to emphasize what the initial disciples of Jesus felt: whenever food passed through their Master's hands, there was always enough. In the circle of Jesus, no one went hungry. No one got more than their share. Like manna, Jesus bread was the quintessential symbol of God's distributive justice. "Enough."

In our time we still gather each Sabbath and when we recite the Lord's Prayer we ask God for this special bread. Translated into modern parlance, it might sound like this: "Give us enough for today." Having "enough" is a dream of the destitute because they never get it. But "enough" is a nightmare for those people who have too much. How can we survive if all we have is just a single day's worth of nourishment? When you've enjoyed owning and eating a full loaf, it feels like an undesirable descent to have only a few crusts.

This is the problem of the gap between our context and that of the gospel. Jesus was speaking out of a context of scarcity. It is hard for those who are accustomed to abundance to hear the message. In fact, "enough" is an insult, an invitation to insanity in a culture of extravagance. We want more. We desire excess—just to be secure, to be somebody.

Wouldn't many church-goers lose substantial slices of their standard of living if all they ate was their share? "Give us this day our daily bread?" It's the most disturbing prayer I can imagine. In the well-healed world such a petition begins to feel more like punishment than benediction. Are we being asked to relinquish our excesses, the nest eggs we've built up as protection against future contingencies? Yes! Given the logic of manna in the wilderness, Jesus is calling us to that sacred place where we take only our portion—insuring that the surplus is available for those who don't have enough.

Strip away all the slogans and gimmicks and Christian discipleship stands on the simple practice of saying "enough is enough."

Day 14:
The Full Meal Deal

Opening Prayer
> *Jesus, you come to me in many disguises—the pan handler, president, and prostitute. Open my eyes to see you.*

John 6:9
> **"There's a lad here with five barley breads and two fish."**

At the heart of the Christian gospel is the central affirmation that Jesus of Nazareth, while fixed in the historical period of first-century Palestine, is still alive. Each day he is born again in the hearts and minds of Christians around the world. Martin Luther, a Christian protester and reformer, used the image of a mirror to describe his Saviour: "Jesus was the Mirror of the fatherly heart."

While Luther may be correct to assert that Jesus embodies the great heart beating behind creation, it is also accurate to assert that Christ is a mirror of the human soul. He reflects back to the devout, their deepest dreams and most frequent fears. And since every culture grows its own language and system of values, Jesus appears in each new society wearing a different face. After 2000 years of devotion, there are as many images of Jesus as there are human hands to hold the mirror of his countenance. To the condemned and guilt-ridden soul, Jesus looks like forgiveness. To the oppressed, he is liberation. Hungry people see him as the bread miracle worker. The affluent acknowledge him as a wise teacher, and the politically active name him "King."

This flexibility of images is not evidence of intellectual uncertainty or spiritual confusion, but a central tenet of the Christian tradition, the truth of incarnation. Jesus is not in static icon, but a dynamic encounter, born anew into each new context.

During his lifetime, the Jesus we know as a spiritual healer and guide was recognized much more as a meal ticket. His companions came from the landless, dispossessed wage labourers, the bottom rung of the social ladder of Galilee. Having no land, these people were without legal status and regarded as socially suspect. It was the land that conferred worth. So these valueless people had to depend on the strength of their hands and the benevolence of landowners for their daily bread. Starvation was just a day's wages away. It was into this reality that Jesus was born and it would be false to imagine him as a first-century professional. He was more like a handyman. The guy who knew how stuff worked—wood, metal or stone. So he was a lot like the landless peasants, lepers, and other rejects who were the doormats of his world.

So when Jesus spoke about bread in a world of scarcity, the spiritual connotations of the word were not the first image people considered. Bread was freedom from want; it was the ticket to living another day. Of course, having daily bread had deep theological implications—but these insights only arise once your belly is full and they last only as long as you can see from whence comes your next meal. This is perhaps the most difficult obstacle for an affluent society to overcome. How do we understand the good news of a gospel of "enough" when we have enjoyed too much for so long?

I'll leave that question with you while we make the bread of a peasant. It is only John's gospel that tells the story of the feeding of the multitudes with a specific bread in mind: barley cakes. It was a complete meal for many peasants. As you eat it, add a little fried fish, and you'll be living the simple life that acts as the backdrop to so many of Jesus' tales.

Barley Cakes

1. Proof 3 tablespoons of yeast in 1 cup of warm water.

2. Mix together 4 cups white flour, 2 cups barley flour, 2 cups whole wheat flour, 1 tablespoon salt, ⅓ cup white sugar.

3. Mix together 1 cup plain yogurt, ½ cup olive oil, ½ cup warm water.

4. When yeast is proofed, mix it with flour and the yogurt/oil/water.

5. Optional: if you want to add more to make this a full meal add some or all of: ⅓ cup chopped pitted olives, ¼ cup chopped sun dried tomatoes, 1 clove garlic crushed, ½ cup chopped feta cheese, ½ cup honey, pinch of cumin, curries, cloves.

6. Knead dough into a slightly sticky consistency for 10 minutes. Let rise for 2 hours.

7. Shape into six round loaves—flatten into 8-inch circles. Brush with olive oil. Let rise for 2 hours.

8. Bake at 350°F for 35–45 minutes or until well browned.

A great bread for lunch: serve with a little soup or fried fish. In the Mediterranean world, it would be dipped in yogurt or hummus as a breakfast meal.

Day 15:
The Perfect Bread

Opening Prayer

> *God of the peasant and president, give me bread for the day that I may eat—calm my stomach to enjoy the daily feast you provide—however it comes.*

Luke 10:7

> **"Stay at that house, eating and drinking whatever they provide."**

A portion of a pastor's time is given to home visits. When I was serving a community of faith, a typical week might involve several visits and I would gauge the quality of our encounter by the level of sustenance we consumed. A cookie was a bite-size portion of intimacy. A complete meal was evidence of a godly connection.

From the parishioner's point of view, putting out a spread for the minister, priest or rabbi has been a time-weathered vehicle for the unburdening of a troubled soul. There is something reassuring about having the spiritual leader's feet under your table, and common food makes confessions possible because it seems to level the spiritual playing field. A shared meal is an invitation to share vulnerability.

When I was a young student minister I was invited to Jud's farm for what he called his special family repast: "Chicken and burgers done to a turn!" I was intrigued. I'd been to his house several times for tea, but never a meal. He lived at the far end of the parish—a difficult spot to reach if I wanted to get back before dark. On the assigned day, having parked the car on the road, I made my way through Jud's farmstead. It was littered with a collection of Saskatchewan's best farm implements, and it was hard to identify what was actually retired from service and what was in active duty. Rust, the great leveller, covered almost everything. The animals, mostly pigs and chickens, found their food and lodging in this jungle of metal. They had fenced off residences, but no one, including the farm family, seemed inclined to respect arbitrary boundaries like corrals, pens or coops.

The sun was hot, and consequently, there wasn't much action in the yard. Pigs slumped under rotting hay wagons—the grass and mud giving some relief. Chickens pecked the parched, but shaded ground beside burnt-out grain trucks. The flies were buzzing everywhere, but even they seemed slower in the heat.

Once we had sat down for the meal, I was presented with a five course feast—mountains of mashed potatoes, buckets of beans and peas, hamburgers to feed a battalion, enough fried chicken to make the Colonel jealous. Even with Jud's crowd of kids, I couldn't imagine how we'd eat even a fraction of the meal.

There seemed to be very little protocol involved. Large portions all round seemed to be the only principle of etiquette. I selected my share and sunk my 18-year old appetite into a hamburger. Using fork and knife I cut a patty in half and as I raised it to my mouth I noticed that a flaked off piece of meat which fell to my plate turned out to be housefly. Mercifully, dead. Obviously this critter had been caught in the cooking and been roasted along with beef. As I munched away, I wondered how many of his comrades might still be lodged in the burger in my mouth.

It was at that moment that I realized eating was a moment of unique vulnerability. At the dinner table there is always a risk of catching someone's sickness, being subject to another person's sense of hygiene. Obviously, Jud didn't worry too much about flies. "Hell, they're trying to make a living like the rest of us." Why should his guests get picky?

Absolute assurance kills the hungry soul. Lower our pretence and we heighten our awareness of God. A common cup is not just a sign of unity, it is the embodiment of trust, the acknowledgment that we risk life's calamities and triumphs together. I swept the fly off my plate and kept chewing. Common meals are invitations from our Creator to relax and get real. Amen!

On the next page is a simple stick bread that is my favourite—the baguette, a bread of great commonality.

French Baguettes

The shaping of this bread may prove to be a challenge. If you're having trouble, try several firm small balls or a larger, fatter loaf.

1. Proof 2 tablespoons of yeast in 1 cup warm water with 1 tablespoon of sugar.

2. Mix yeast with 2 cups white flour, 1 cup warm milk, ½ cup warm water, and 3 teaspoons salt—stir well for 3 minutes. (You'll need a large bread bowl for this.)

3. Add up to 3 cups more of white flour—until the dough pulls away from the sides of the bowl—a good spongy dough. (The liquid to flour match may take practice.)

4. Knead for 10 minutes.

5. Place in greased bowl, cover with damp cloth, place in a cold oven with the light on. Let rise for 1½ hours.

6. Roll out dough into three rectangles, 12 by 15 inches, and then roll them starting on the long side. Make sure you roll the entire edge at the same pace—tightness being the object. Once complete, pinch closed the edges and ends and place the tube-like roll seam down on a greased baking dish (sprinkled with cornmeal) or in French baguette pan (also sprinkled with cornmeal).

7. Paint each loaf with an egg white (mixed with 1 teaspoon water) and let stand in oven with light on for another 45 minutes (or until double).

8. Paint again with egg white mixture (carefully—you don't want to inadvertently punch it down again). Slice the top diagonally with three strokes of a sharp knife.

9. Bake at a 375°F for 30 to 35 minutes.

This recipe uses no oil. So consequently, the bread will dry out quickly. It is best eaten fresh and crispy. An excellent instrument for building common bonds and tearing down social obstacles! The warm milk can be substituted for warm water if you want a drier loaf.

Day 16:
Hanging In

Opening Prayer

When I hurt, save me from self-pity. When I hurt, direct my thoughts to healing and not toward complaining. When I betray my best intentions, direct my steps toward my responsibility.

Matthew 6:26

"Take a look at the birds of the sky; they don't plant or harvest or gather into barns. Yet your heavenly Father feeds them. You're worth more than they, aren't you?"

It wasn't until I put the second to last sheet of tin on the roof that I discovered my problem. Hanging on with my right hand, while the left was wielding an electric drill, I thought back over the steps that had brought me to this predicament. The instructions tucked into the package had been simple: placing each course of screw nails two feet apart, work your way out from freshly installed sheets across the old covering. "Be careful not to walk across the tin once it has been attached to the roofing surface." Having read through the first seven of 14 "helpful hints" for correct installation, I went at the job with great energy and abandon. So far so good. Except, the well blocked, tied, and tethered ladder was now on the wrong side of my tin. Leave me hanging there for a moment and we'll start a North American bread recipe:

Anadama bread—the best toast going. Mix 3 tablespoons yeast with a cup of warm water and a tablespoon of sugar. Let stand while you stir 2½ cups boiling water into a cup of cornmeal, 4 tablespoons of butter or margarine, a tablespoon of salt, and ¾ cup of molasses. Let cool.

I had built myself into a corner. Should I jump the 12 feet down? I could feel my grip slipping. The light dusting of water under my feet was reducing friction. I didn't have a lot of time to decide what to do. But as in most emergency situations, a number of pictures flashed before my eyes. There was Chuck, who had just this last month graduated from a walker to crutches. He was hoping to be free of all appliances within a year and that would be a miracle since initially the doctors said he would never get out of a wheelchair. Chuck had fallen off his garage roof.

Your yeast is now ready, so add it to 8 cups of flour and then add the cooled to warm molasses cornmeal mixture. (Be careful that it is not too hot or it will kill the yeast.) Mix into spongy dough and knead for 10 minutes.

Then there was David, my father-in-law, who had taken a swan dive off his house roof. Again, it was simple job. Just checking the flashing under his living room eve. To add injury to insult, the loader had fallen on top of him and practically broken his back. He broke his nose and jaw, and nearly killed himself.

Roofs are dangerous slopes, especially when they slip out from under you. From Chuck to David, I went immediately to my Creator. Not that I was praying for a miracle. Rather, I was struck by the thought of the slender thread that attaches us to life. One misstep and I might be finished.

I know the terror of watching my three-year old balancing precariously on the swing set around the corner at the park. He leaps from platform to pole, slithers around plastic tunnels, swings down ropes, and generally sends my heart into my mouth a dozen times a minute. If I know the fear and helplessness of a father who watches his offspring testing his wings, how much more does our Maker suffer through the tribulations of her children. Imagine carrying the weight of all the world's people—each one precious and particular. Surely this is evidence of a tremendous love.

Let the assurance of this love spill over your soul as you finish kneading. Then cover the dough with a damp tea towel in a greased bowl for 2 hours. Shape into 3 loaves and bake at 350° for 45 minutes.

Often believers impute supreme power to their God, unfathomable wisdom and eternal spirit, but in comparison to the love of a parent, these other attributes are pale. A mother who watches her children go off to school, knowing that she is unable to protect them from all the bumps and bruises of the schoolyard has mountains more courage. She willingly accepts the vulnerability and weakness of loving hoping they will be all right. How much more impressive is the Lord of Life who embraces all creatures with this helpless love!

I was caught with the awe of my Creator's love when a friend walked around the corner of the shed carrying a ladder. "Thought you might need a hand," he shouted up to me. Who said God is dead? I can see him standing below me in blue jeans and a T-shirt that reads, "No fear."

Anadama Bread

1. Mix 3 tablespoons yeast with 1 cup warm water and 1 tablespoon sugar.

2. Let stand while you stir 2½ cups boiling water into 1 cup of cornmeal, 4 tablespoons butter or margarine, 1 tablespoon salt, and ¾ cup molasses. Let cool.

3. Add yeast to 8 cups flour and then add cooled molasses and cornmeal mixture.

4. Mix into spongy dough and knead for 10 minutes.

5. Cover dough with damp tea towel in a greased bowl for 2 hours.

6. Shape into 3 loaves and bake at 350°F for 45 minutes.

The Third Sunday in Lent:
A Sabbatical Summary

Opening Prayer
God of the wilderness, fill all people with bread. Rain down on all creatures their just share of your blessings.

John 6:35
Jesus explained to them, "I am the bread of life."

No bread making today. Just a story.

An atheist was taking a walk through the woods, admiring all that the "accident of evolution" had created. "What majestic trees! What powerful rivers! What beautiful animals!" he said to himself.

As he walked alongside the river, he heard a rustling in the bushes behind him. Turning to look, he saw an enormous grizzly charging toward him. He ran as fast as he could up the path. After several breathless seconds he looked over his shoulder and alas, the bear was gaining on him. So he tried to move more quickly, but as he glanced back again, the great beast was drawing even closer. His heart was pumping frantically as he tried to push himself faster, faster. Just then, he tripped and fell to the ground. Rolling to pick himself up, he saw the gigantic bear right on top of him raising a paw for the killer blow. At that instant the atheist cried out, "Oh my God, save me!"

Immediately, time stopped. A trumpet blared, the bear froze, the forest was silent, the river even stopping moving. A bright light shone upon the man, and a voice came out of the sky saying, "You have denied my existence all of these years. You have taught others I don't exist, even credited my creation to a cosmic accident, and now you expect me to help you out of this predicament. Am I to count you as a believer now, a true follower of Jesus?"

The atheist looked into the light and said, "It would be rather hypocritical to ask to be a Christian after all these years, but could you make the bear a Christian?"

"Very well," said the voice.

Instantly, the light went out, the river ran, and the sounds of the forest continued, but the bear lowered his long claws and bringing both his paws together, he bowed his head and said: "Lord Jesus, I thank you for this food, which I am about to receive."

Strange things happen when we introduce the name of Jesus into daily living. Suddenly, the horns of heaven sound, and we start to hear angelic voices—we're transported to a place above this earth. Jesus! It's almost impossible to get behind the magic and might of Messiah worship to uncover the peasant carpenter of Galilee. He's become so much of a spiritual icon that we can't meet him as a fellow human being any longer! His bread is the miraculous medicine of immortality.

Yet, his bread is first of all real bread—food for the hungry, a symbol and an embodiment of God's distributive justice. In God's realm everyone has enough—not too much and not too little. Enough!

Day 17:
Bread of Rejoicing

Opening Prayer
God of the party and the feast, shape my joy this day.

Luke 15:23-24
"...Let's have a feast and celebrate, because this son of mine was dead and has come back to life; he was lost and now is found."

I have never known a more spiritual invitation than: "Let's eat!" Eating has always been a central religious act. No matter what the tradition, the shared meal, either in the form of a symbolic banquet or a dinner, has been a key element in the search for and adoration of God.

Taking nourishment is a daily festival, the hallowing of life. Why shouldn't eating find a central place in public worship? It underlines the "joy to the world" that God has given to all creatures. But alas, the worshipful, pleasure-filled abandonment of eating, while it is present in certain faith communities has been lost to modern Christians. We have forgotten the roots of our own soul-food meal—the Last, the Lord's Supper.

I can recall when I was a child the days when our church celebrated the sacrament of the upper room. Entering the sanctuary I would first see a white shawl spilled over the communion table on all sides. It looked like a flag-draped coffin. A sombre atmosphere hung over the entire service like the noxious fumes of recent forest fires. Snickers were smothered. Smiles were erased. This was no frivolous party, but serious business. Once the starched linen was removed, and this was done with great solemnity, Court Fissette and Harold Orr, the two chief elders in my church, would carefully remove silver lids and arrange trays of bread. They looked like they were uncovering their best friend's closest secrets. When all was set, my father would intone the immortal words: "Do this in remembrance of me." After some time I realized that we were re-enacting an ancient memorial service—the last rites for Jesus. Grim faced elders soberly passed small crumbs and crusts to the hushed crowd. "The bread of life," they whispered. Heads were bowed. Silence reigned. The trays of tiny clinking glasses went up and down the pews. A small shot glass for every disciple. We each sipped a thimbleful of grape juice. "The promise of a new heaven come to earth."

There was certainty dignity and ritual in that symbolic supper. Any meal requires both. You can't just slap down a can of beans with a fork and hope that a dinner will have elegance and flavour. But what a parsimonious repast! And where was the revelling in the fruits of creation? A close reading of the Christian sacrament reveals that it was more than an act of remembrance. It was also a foretaste of a great feast to come when all people will share a common table—the messianic banquet. No one will be excluded, and there will be bowls of abundance and platters of plenty. No one will be hungry when they leave that special spread. At this meal there will be laughter and rejoicing for it is our opportunity to tell the stories of God's salvation.

If there is any aspect of the Christian tradition I would like to re-introduce into public worship, it would be the love and taste of a shared meal, and not just on Saturday night at the potluck. Surely, a feast on a Sunday morning would revitalize our faith as it nourishes our bodies. To those who hunger for spirit, depth, and substance, there could be no more fitting invocation than, "Let's eat!"

Here's a bagel recipe that corresponds to the festive delights of the great banquet our Maker sets for us.

Bagels

1. Take 2 level tablespoons of dry yeast, 1 teaspoon of sugar, and ½ cup of warm water, and mix it together. Let it stand for 10 minutes.

2. Put 8 cups of white flour, ¼ cup of sugar and ½ cup olive oil, and 1½ tablespoons of salt in a bowl. Mix in 2 cups of warm water. Stir in whole eggs.

3. Once yeast is foamy, stir it into the flour mixture and start kneading.

4. Knead for 10 to 15 minutes. (If your dough is still stiff add a tad more water; a touch more flour if it's still sticking to your hands.)

5. Roll it into a ball and plop it into a greased bread bowl. Then cover with a damp cloth.

6. Two hours later, tip it out onto a floured counter, shape 30 balls, and let stand for 10 minutes.

7. Heat 8 cups water and ⅛ cup of sugar (not boiling).

8. Using index finger and thumb pinch a hole in each ball. Twirl the dough around your index finger until a large hole is made and you have an evenly shaped bagel.

9. Place 4 to 5 shaped bagels into the heated water—cover for 3½ minutes and then flip for 3½ more minutes.

10. Preheat oven to 375°F.

11. Roll the "boiled" bagels in poppy or sesame seeds and then bake for 35–45 minutes. (I use greased small cookie sheets for the baking. Ideally you can fit two onto each rack of the oven since you'll have to add new "boiled" bagels while the first batch bakes. It's tricky—you can't leave the kitchen while making bagels.)

12. Cool. Then create a feast with cream cheese and jam.

Bagels have a chewy texture because of the water bath. For more varieties add any of following combinations before you knead the dough (but for these varieties don't dip the bagels in seeds as mentioned above).

1. ½ cup raisins, a teaspoon each of cinnamon and nutmeg

2. 1½ cups sharp cheese and ½ cup fresh chives

3. 1 cup sun dried tomatoes, one crushed clove of garlic, and ½ cup white onion

4. 1 cup hot salsa (shred 1 cup cheddar cheese over boiled bagels before baking)

Day 18:
Grandma Lloyd's Gift of Touch

Opening Prayer

God of grain and grape, when I am hungry, feed me, when I am lost, bring me home, and when I am cowering, stand by me 'til I rise up.

Matthew 6:34

"So don't fret about tomorrow. Let tomorrow fret about itself. The troubles that the day brings are enough."

A recent edition of *Ladies Home Journal*[3] listed 10 things everyone should know about kissing. For instance, were you aware that the record for the longest kiss is held by Mark and Roberta Griswold of Allen Park, Michigan? They achieved that notable honour by locking lips continuously for 29 hours back in 1998. For the weight conscious, here's a vital piece of information: a passionate kiss uses 6.4 calories per minute. In the same article, there was also a piece of history about the origins of the "French kiss." In the 1920s a prudish American culture thought the citizens of France were over-sexed and spoke of anything beyond a respectful peck on the lips as a "French kiss."

Well there were a number of other tidbits about kissing, but the final note in the article caught my attention: during a single chaste kiss as many as 278 colonies of bacteria are exchanged between kissee and kissor. I began to perceive that this profound fact might explain one of the central dimensions of Anglo-Cannuck culture—our standoffishness. No exchange of germs please, we're the True North Strong and Frozen. Our brothers and sisters from Quebec cast caution to the wind and do a double kiss twice in any serious encounter, once on each cheek when you

---

3. February 2000, p. 18.

come in the door, and again when you leave. (Some tropical cultures have a "three peck" prerogative that accompanies every human encounter.)

Canadians are not mushy feely types. The bacteria not withstanding, we don't touch each other often. In a study of such matters it was determined that in a regular one-hour lunch in Acapulco, Mexicans touch each other an average of 110 times. Parisians are a tad bit less demonstrative, but still comfortable in their bodies—making contact over 33 times in the same 60 minutes. Americans—especially from the deep south—touch at least once in their lunch time encounters. But Canadians—we didn't even make it onto the touch scale. Add to this sorry cultural heritage a heightened awareness and apprehension of unwanted physical contact and you have a double barrier. When I teach ethics to M.B.A. students, one of the principles I now suggest for employer—employee relationships is "no touching" of any kind, ever. It's a sad state of affairs (necessary perhaps, but sad nonetheless) when we transform ourselves into a community of untouchables.

Now, into this mix I introduce Grandma Lloyd, a woman who through many adverse life experiences had the gift of touch. It wasn't physical—she was still a reserved Canadian after all—but she touched her loved ones with her cooking and kindness: she turned the meal into a circle where all had a place, food was plentiful, and no one was left out. If there was a miracle of the first Jesus circle, it was this touch ability. In a society that had rigid and high boundaries, the carpenter of Nazareth worked miracles of healing through shared bread.

Here's Grandma Lloyd's own recipe for sharing—a breakfast delight that is light and sweet.

Grandma Lloyd's Scones

1. Mix together 2 cups flour, 2½ teaspoons baking powder, a pinch of salt, ⅓ cup of sugar.

2. Cut ½ cup butter or margarine into the flour mixture until it is small granules.

3. Add 1 whole egg and ⅓ cup milk.

4. Mix until a stiffened ball is formed. Flatten on a floured surface into a 9-inch round and cut into 8 pieces. (Optional: brush the pieces with egg whites and sprinkle sugar over top.)

5. Place on a greased cookie sheet and into the oven at 350°F for 15 minutes.

6. Serve with butter and jam—a touching feast if ever there was one.

I usually bake these in the morning for breakfast. Add cheese and coffee and you're in paradise! For tea biscuits, reduce the amount of sugar by half and enjoy a tarter flavour for lunch times with hot soup or afternoon snacks on the back deck.

The Third Ingredient of Daily Bread Discipleship:

Bread as Acceptance

Day 19:
Ostrich Eggs and Bantam Hens

Opening Prayer
> *God, help me to accept the unacceptable, to touch the untouchable, to make a place when the table is crowded, and to know that at your meal, all are welcome.*

Luke 4:16-19
> When he came to Nazareth, where he had been brought up, he went to the synagogue on the Sabbath day, as was his custom. He stood up to do the reading and was handed the scroll of the prophet Isaiah. He unrolled the scroll and found the place where it was written:
>> "The Spirit of the Lord is upon me
>> because he has anointed me
>> to bring good news to the poor.
>> He has sent me to announce pardon for prisoners
>> and recovery of sight to the blind;
>> To set free the oppressed,
>> to proclaim the year of the Lord's amnesty."

The great Protestant Reformer, John Calvin, once said that too much Christian preaching is like holding up an ostrich egg to a company of bantam hens and saying, "Well, do your best." Is that how you feel when you go to church or think of the religious life—battered by impossible imperatives? How many devout hearts are broken on the reefs of these great expectations? There is no question that many earnest people turn away from religious institutions because they feel they are unworthy.

This is a pity since the sincere of heart are everywhere searching for a religious tradition that will help them to integrate their spiritual quest with their daily routine. There's no question that having worthy goals that lie beyond our grasp is a heavenly virtue, but I want to offer another approach. Instead of the ostrich-egg-and-bantam-hen theology, how about doing what we can with what we have where we are?

At first glance, this may appear to be a defeatist attitude—allowing people off the ethical hook. But on second thought, it seems of little use to the world if we hold off acting in a just manner until we're trained fully to be prophets. There doesn't have to be any blinding light or miraculous moment. The opportunities to be engaged in God's reign on earth are waiting the moment you open your eyes.

The story of Dietrich Bonhoeffer is an eloquent example of doing what you can with what you have where you are. He was a Christian pastor in the confessing church in Germany during World War II. Jews came to his manse seeking refuge, and he smuggled them out of the country. His friends drew him into resistance, and even though he was at heart a pacifist, he participated in the plot to assassinate Hitler. Eventually he was arrested for his actions. In the dark shadows of his cell-block, he felt a great helplessness. His family's work to rescue Jews was beyond his reach, and the resistance could hardly afford to communicate with him. It looked like his usefulness was past, but he could still write letters and that he did. Hundreds of messages streamed from the various Gestapo holding tanks where he was lodged: words for a baptismal service, a homily for a marriage ceremony, greetings for family, words of encouragement to friends, and love letters to his fiancée.

In one of the last letters he wrote before he was executed, Bonhoeffer spoke of a conversation with a priest who argued that the point of a religious life was to attain sainthood. Bonhoeffer replied, "I discovered ...and am still discovering...that it is only by living completely in this world that one learns to have faith. One must completely abandon any attempt to make something of oneself, whether it be a saint or converted sinner....By this worldliness, I mean living unreservedly in life's duties, problems, successes and failures, experiences and perplexities. In so doing we throw ourselves completely into the arms of God, taking seriously, not our own suffering, but those of God in the world."

When Jesus broke bread with his followers, the message was similar: "Leave off attempts at sainthood. Away with the ostrich eggs. Offer your Creator the best you have, and it will be enough."

Day 20:
Will the Real Zacchaeus Please Stand Up?

Opening Prayer
> *Save me…keep me from my best ideas, the polite absolutes that have blinded me to who is actually before me. Open my hands to embrace the ones I have ignored, blamed or scorned.*

Luke 19:1-2
> **Then he entered Jericho and was making his way through it. Now a man named Zacchaeus lived there who was head toll collector and a rich man.**

In Christian circles, the name Zacchaeus is synonymous with the call of repentance. He was a sinner, a cheat, and a devious man. But in the account of Luke's gospel, this lowly creature's encounter with Jesus becomes a life-altering experience. Charles Dickens couldn't have done better. The grizzly miser mends his ways and embraces the poor and destitute that surround him. That's the traditional word on Zacchaeus, but what if Zacchaeus isn't who we think he is? Perhaps the portrait of the repentant sinner has more to do with religious self-interest than clear biblical truth. Here's why an alternative reading is possible.

The story, found only in Luke's gospel, contains a cryptic phrase in (chapter 19) verse 9. It says, "He stood his ground." Now the tale begins with Zacchaeus literally up a tree, wanting to catch a glimpse of this new rabbi. Once Jesus reaches this spot, he looks up and calls to the tax collector, inviting him to come down since they are going to dine together. This is where the crowd scene starts.

In a typical reaction, the mob starts to grumble, unsettled by Jesus' unorthodox meal etiquette. He's always eating and carousing with "bad" people—the kind we'd rather see behind bars than across the table. So these "good" folk stand outside the home of the tax collector, tisk-tisking, until the meal is over. When they emerge, Zacchaeus "stood his ground" and says that if he has cheated anyone he'll repay them four-fold, and as proof he'll give half of all that he possesses to the impoverished.

But why would Zacchaeus need to "stand his ground" unless he was defending himself? Centuries of interpretation have linked the reference to the ground and the short man clambering down from the sycamore tree. Even though the two ideas are separated by lunch, we linked them to fabricate a much-desired conversion.

So if Zacchaeus is defending himself, could he be someone who has no reason to fear the grunts and groans of his community? What if he is a rich, righteous man who has been the subject of communal prejudice? What would it mean, if he is, as his name suggests, a righteous man? (That's what *Zacchaeus* means. "Pure one.") Maybe he's not a repentant cheat, but a compassionate fair believer.

Luke loves reversals—the Good Samaritan is another example. Here in the nineteenth chapter we are confronted by our own religious bias— wanting a sinner, we act just like the gossips in Jericho. Many of the Jesus encounters have an ironic twist. As in this case, it is the very people who think they are "good" that aren't, and the folks we have decided are the "unwashed untouchables" turn out to be virtuous.

The second function of bread-breaking in the circle of Jesus was to dispel our spiritual distinctions—no one is better, no one is shunned, everyone is welcome at his table. Our world is splintering all too easily into ethnic and spiritual camps, each wrapping itself in ultimate truth. We pitch insults and ignorance at each other from the safe haven of our bigotry. Yet, as the globe shrinks, we can no longer afford these Zacchaeus-like slurs. It's time for face-to-face encounters, to embrace our detractors with the joyous and open spirit that seems to characterize this tax collector character.

Day 21:
Childish Fear

Opening Prayer
> *I am afraid that I don't measure up—a failure and flop at the religious game. I will never be allowed into the inner circle.*
> *Help me!*

Matthew 9:10
> **And it so happened while he was dining in Matthew's house that many toll collectors and sinners showed up just then, and they dined with Jesus and his disciples.**

Bread is more than bread.

Meal times in the Palestinian world were events of vulnerability when sin could be transferred along with contagion. Given a common bowl and the lack of utensils and discrete individual portions, there was considerable attention paid to the guest list at any formal dinner. Your guests would have their hands in your food! The best spiritual common sense told people of that time that you shouldn't eat with sinners—you might catch their disease.

Jesus broke with this closed practice and opened up his table— breaking bread with anyone. In the process he confronted religious prejudice and childish apprehension.

A couple had two little boys ages 8 and 10, who were prone to acts of mischief—each spurring the other on to greater acts of delinquency. Consequently, they were always getting into trouble. Alas, their reputations preceded them so that if any mischief occurred in their town, they were blamed even if they weren't involved. Naturally the boys' parents were beside themselves with fretting. "Will they ever grow up?" they moaned to each other as they curled up on the couch late at night. There seemed to be no punishment or disciplinary idea they had not tried.

Then the mother heard that a clergyman in town had been successful in disciplining children, so she asked if he would speak with her boys. The cleric agreed, but asked to see them individually. So the eight-year-old was dutifully sent first in the morning. The prelate agreed to interview the older boy in the afternoon.

This minister was a huge man with a booming voice and when the young boy came to his office, he asked him to sit. Once arranged the small boy looked up to his elder, trying to appear obedient and interested. The clergyman asked sternly, "Where is God?" The boy's mouth dropped open, but he made no response. He sat wide eyed with his jaw gaping. So the minister repeated the question in an even sterner tone, "Where is God?" Again the lad made no attempt to answer. Turning purple, the clergyman raised his voice even more and shook his finger in the boy's face bellowing, "WHERE IS GOD?" The boy screamed and bolted from the room, ran directly home, and dove into his closet, slamming the door behind him.

The older brother, apprehensive about his turn in the minister's clutches, went after his younger sibling and found him hiding behind boxes and garbage bags of used clothes—shaking. "What happened?" he asked. The younger brother, gasping for breath and close to tears, replied, "We are in BIG trouble this time. God is missing—and they think WE did it!"

It's just a story, a funny tale—but there was a time in our lives when we shook with fear because we had run afoul of the religious police, knowing we weren't acceptable. Do you recall that incident? You could feel a knot forming in your stomach—God had you in his clutches. Your mouth went dry as the hot wrath of the Almighty blew your way.

Jesus calms those storms and spreads a meal for everyone—not compelling, but inviting, not excluding, but embracing. "There's a place at the table for you—leave your fear at the door. You are always welcome here."

Day 22:
Fast Food

Opening Prayer
Fill us. Bring us bread that truly satisfies—your loaves of acceptance where all are welcomed. God, give these to your people.

Mark 8:6-8
Then he [Jesus] orders the crowd to sit down on the ground. And he took the seven loaves, gave thanks, and broke them into pieces and started giving [them] to his disciples to hand out; and they passed them around to the crowd....They had more than enough to eat.

Something happens to food when it becomes "fast." I spent a week travelling the Trans-Canada Highway, and the only source of edibles to be found along the highway were the "fast-food" chains. After a few days of trying the many meal deals, it became clear that the only distinction between the outlets was the wrapping; it always tasted the same.

Apart from taste, when food becomes "fast," we lose its essential quality. A meal is not just the regular intake of essential nutrient groups. Like many cultures, we use our dining rooms as bonding spaces. Even in this don't-bother-me-Jack culture, we still feel that friendship is never really cemented until we've put our feet under the same table. What else is the power-lunch all about except establishing a common bond through food? We could easily and more inexpensively carry on our business in little cubicles, inject ourselves with sufficient nourishment to satisfy the noon hour peckishness, and get on with the day's activities. Why stop?

Breaking bread together makes a non-verbal commitment. It's a way to be open to one another, to embrace an element of vulnerability, and establish trust. And it takes time. The longer we spend at the table, the better chances we have of making the meal magic work.

At this time of year, Christians and Jews think about eating a lot. For the Hebraic world it is the Seder, for the Christians the Last or Lord's Supper. In both instances there is a centrality given to bread and wine, but that's where the similarity ends. The Seder is a joyous celebration recounting God's action in history. The Christian sacrament is more sombre, centred largely on a memorial feast commemorating the crucifixion of Jesus and a new covenant made by his sacrifice. There is a connection between these two meals (some scholars suggest that the Lord's Supper arose out of the Seder meal). Jesus may have taken elements from that traditional feast and adapted them for his own ritual, but I believe the bread and wine sacrament of the Christian tradition was a ritualized and reduced version of the larger meal practice of Jesus.

We know that when the carpenter from Galilee travelled through peasant villages, his *modus operandi* was to heal the sick and in return to receive the hospitality of the local villagers—a common meal. But it was not an ordinary feast. The Rabbi of Nazareth brought together a range of people who would never have sat down to the communal serving dish as a group. When Jesus was presiding, sinners and saints dipped their hands into the same bowl.

It is difficult for people today to see what a radical step Jesus was taking in opening up his table to all comers. By bringing widely divergent segments of society together to eat a common meal, he was living out a covenantal relationship where everyone had a place. No one got too much, and everyone was accepted. God came alive in their midst as they shared their common need for sustenance.

I might suggest that all too often the current liturgical practice of the Lord's Supper is to that original Jesus fellowship what fast food is to Sunday dinner. The institution of a priestly controlled and highly symbolic meal has abbreviated and therefore undermined the original intention of the sacrament. It wasn't about "a magic" performed by a single person who was set aside for the role of presider. The shared meal was the great leveller. And it never pretended about nourishment. A crumb of bread and a drop of wine can hardly compare with a life-giving meal where everyone is fed regardless of race, religion, or gender.

It is to the credit of the Christian church that it is weaning itself from this diet of fast food. Let's get back to the real meal deal!

The Fourth Sunday in Lent:
A Sabbatical Summary

Opening Prayer
> *God of the outcast, open my heart to see you among the rejects and losers, the lost and lamenting of this world.*

John 6:35
> **Jesus explained to them, "I am the bread of life. Anyone who comes to me will never be hungry again, and anyone who believes in me will never again be thirsty."**

Another day off. Besides the insight that Jesus used bread as bread, food for the body, what else is obvious about his use of broken loaves? Didn't he use a common meal as a visible and tangible message of acceptance? Everyone around the table was welcome. The outcasts were brought home. The lost were found. It was a simple miracle, but one that has stood the test of time. Breaking bread is more than physical sustenance. It is a clear word of invitation. "Let's eat" can also be translated as "You are loveable and worthy." A simple message—one we can let sink in as we try the following bread.

Cheese Bread

1. Take 2 level tablespoons of dry yeast, a teaspoon of sugar, and ½ cup of warm water, and mix it together. Let it stand for 10 minutes.

2. Put 8 cups of white flour, ⅓ cup each of sugar and olive oil, 1 tablespoon of salt in a bowl. Mix in 2½ cups of warm water. (2 eggs are optional.)

3. Once yeast is foamy, stir it into the flour mixture and start kneading.

4. Knead for 10 to 15 minutes. (If your dough is still stiff, add a tad more water; a touch more flour if it's sticking to your hands.)

5. Roll it into a ball and plop it into a greased bread bowl. Then cover with a damp cloth.

6. Two hours later, tip it out onto a floured counter and shape into 36 small balls.

7. Place a layer of balls in each of two, well-greased loaf pans, then pack with ¼ pound of sharp cheddar cheese. Add a second layer of balls and cover with ¼ pound of sharp cheese.

8. Allow 2–2½ hours more to rise. Then bake at 325°F for 45 minutes. (Temperature 325°–375°F, depending on your oven.)

The cheese bread recipe can be adapted in two ways: change the cheese according to desired taste or work the cheese right into the dough during the first mixing and kneading. This latter method tends to make the bread less piquant, but smoother.

Day 23:
The Ones We Don't See

Opening Prayer

Are there times when we don't see you God, when your ragged clothes and starving gaze masks your majesty? Heaven help us that we should presume to know you in all of your disguises. Keep us from that blasted pretence and keep our eyes attentive to embrace you when you call!

Matthew 25:44

Then they will give him a similar reply: "Lord, when did we notice that you were hungry or thirsty or a foreigner or naked or ill or in prison and did not attempt to help you?"

God is often hidden—not sitting in the splendour of our sanctuaries, but clothed in human misery.

Living in a fertile region of Costa Rica, Alex has been a plantation worker for years. Apart from being a handyman around the village, doing the odd jobs that small industries require, he cuts sugar cane. Breaking a Latin stereotype, Alex takes no mid-day siesta breaks and he works harder than most. When he was younger, he bought a piece of swamp from the local parish council and excavated the entire lot to a depth of six feet—by hand. He then drained the land and built his family home, no small feat in a climate that melts the soul in humidity and heat.

When the cutting season arrives, Alex gathers with the other workers at the head of the forest of canes. There, he is quoted a price for his day's efforts. Each labourer has a section of the crop to harvest and almost before the boss turns his back, the workers are off like a shot, hacking away for all they're worth. It's back breaking work. There is little time for a refreshment break or idle speculation on safety standards. Alex, like the others, knows that the stipulated daily wage is paid to the one lucky worker who finishes his quota of plants first. Those who come after get paid progressively less and less, until the one who finishes last gets nothing. When he first began this career, there were many days when Alex would travel back to his household with nothing to show but a sore back and withered pride.

"That's unjust," you might say and you'd be right, but this tight-fisted competition is the name of the game in this large-scale export market. If you are neither the trans-national company that controls the domestic sugar harvest nor the North American based distributor who sets prices, you're largely powerless. The owners of this refined product rule the bottom line. People like Alex are just a pair of strong arms. There are no unemployment safety nets, welfare is non-existent, and there is no compensation paid for injury or lack of work. You live and all too often starve on what you bring home from the day's labour.

Alex is one of the millions of "untouchables" in our new world economy—the invisible people who are excluded from our meal fellowship. As long as these folk are excluded from their just place at our table, so also is God.

Day 24:
Open Eyes

Opening Prayer
> *God, teach me to see you even when others don't or won't.*

Matthew 7:15
> **Be on the lookout for phony prophets....**

Share in the Jesus meal, and your eyes are opened to the false distinctions we make—how propriety and privilege, creations of human hands, have been exalted to unassailable heights.

The Qur'an tells a story of Abraham before he left his father's house to found a new people and religion. According to the legend, Abe's dad was an idol maker using wood, stone, and whatever and whomever the market dictated. It was a lucrative business. Young Abraham grew up in a culture that venerated these inert objects, and all kinds of gods of great power and promise were shaped in that little shop. Abraham's father was the consummate artisan, treating his creations with utmost sanctity. "These are inspirations of the heavens," he admonished his son apprentice. "The gods guide my hands so that their likeness will be rendered faithfully."

Around Abraham's house there was never any question. The world was governed by many gods, and most of them came from the old man's shop.

One day Abraham senior went off to another village on business, leaving the youngster in charge of the shop. Abe saw his chance. Grasping an axe he whirled his weight into all the idols, splinters, chips, and dust flying in all directions. Eventually they were almost all smashed and broken. Abraham wasn't God's chosen one for nothing for he left a single idol intact, the big one located in the middle of the shop. And then, he waited for daddy to return.

When the old man entered his shop, dismay and horror ranged across his face. Riot, robbery, chaos, anarchy, all these excuses played in his mind, but he could only utter, "Who...who did this?"

Abraham was smug. Pointing to the one idol still standing, he said, "That one did it."

His father flew into a rage and without thinking shouted, "What do you mean? 'He did it!' He is only wood and stone, he can't do anything!"

"Exactly!" Abraham replied.

Next day, having grown up, Abraham left home.

Day 25:
Small Band, Large Work

Opening Prayer

*Lift our hands, move our hearts—to feed those who come to our
door, hungry in body and soul.*

Mark 8:4

**And his disciples answered him, "How can anyone feed
these people out here in this desolate place?"**

There are still Anglophone communities in Quebec. One such
community is located near Percé Rock on the Gaspé Peninsula. It's called
Rosebridge and has a white clapboard United Church and bell tower
that overlook the sea. Adorned by weeping willows and rosebushes, the
structure is postcard perfect. It sits in the middle of a neatly trimmed
cemetery and is home to a faithful band of devout families. Generations
of back-sliding Lelacheurs and born again Langlois have warmed the
pews in that sanctuary.

Mostly fishers and farmers, the Rosebridge congregation has supplied
this land with all kinds of sinners, soldiers, and saints. But alas, as coastal
resources decline and the opportunities for unilingual young people
evaporate, so the English-speaking population dwindles. High school
graduation is more than a rite of passage, it's a ticket to the job-rich cities
of Ontario or Alberta. Nevertheless, this small company of Christians
boasts one of the best strawberry festivals in the region. No matter the
linguistic barriers, the whole community comes out for whipped cream
and freshly baked biscuits.

When I was first told that the local church would feed 500 people at
their strawberry social, I was dumbfounded. How could the scattering of
seniors that faced me from the oak pews of that tiny chapel ever expect to
muster the person power necessary for such a feast? They could hardly
make it up the front steps without help! But no amount of hand wringing

on my part could dissuade them. Even as the great day dawned I had my doubts. I could picture line-ups of hungry citizens complaining about the snail paced service as our half dozen souls served people into the wee small hours. But as the sun rose, so did the list of volunteers. Folks from everywhere arrived to lend a hand. Names that lay dormant, permanently fixed on the inactive side of the membership roster, suddenly sprang to life to lend a hand. Food made sense, as worship did not.

I was left to puzzle, why? Why would agnostics, atheists, and non-attenders show up to help at a church social? Sure, the baking was to die for, and there's nothing like a mound of strawberries as an excuse to eat a bowl brimming with whipped cream! But there was more at play. A common table speaks to most folk, whether they are religious or not, because a meal is the moment when we all admit we are needy creatures. In contrast to the battlefield, senate chamber, or even church chancel, the dining room is a great leveller. It's a humbling environment where, above all else, we admit we are mortal.

It is not strange to associate eating with faithfulness. In consuming food, we acknowledge that there is a Creator who provides for us. No one by dint of virtue or strength of character can instigate the miracle of the harvest. It comes from on high.

In a similar fashion, the exercise of consuming food re-enforces that all beings are equal before God. There is no one who is beyond eating or freed from the necessity of daily bread. Call it solidarity or fellowship, a meal binds us together as children of the Almighty as almost no other activity can.

In the end, we filled 632 plates that season and through the laughter that ran around the hall, I could hear the voice of a spirit that had rarely visited our Sunday morning worship. It was in those flashes of joy, the exuberance of a real meal, where there was a place set for everyone and seconds for any who wanted them, that God came to supper.

Day 26:
The Lenten Dietary Fear—Gluttony

Opening Prayer

> *Give me this day my daily bread. Keep me from taking more than I need.*

Mark 10:23

> **And looking around, Jesus says to his disciples, "How difficult it is for those who have money to enter God's domain."**

Take a Bible study of 10 Christians, stir in the subject of the "seven deadly sins," and what words come out? "Gluttony and lawless," says the first participant. The next retorts, "Sloth and sex." That brings hoots of laughter. Others suggest "bad," or "evil," or "the opposite of virtue." "Greed" is mentioned several times. One member of the circle says "boring." That caught us off guard. Apparently she was recalling the time when a local preacher took up the subject of the seven deadly sins in a series of sermons, but she missed the "juicy ones" and was only present for those sins that seemed less dramatic.

In this the time of Lent, believers have traditionally reflected on their misdeeds and unearthed actions for which they should repent. In that spirit, and at the risk of being boring, but to dispel misconceptions about the biblical understanding of "sin," allow me to explore one sin, gluttony.

Unlike the other mortal misdemeanours, over-eating is a North American temptation. We all know it first-hand for it is a sin associated with excess. The Canadian Broadcasting Corporation recently reported on research involving overweight Canadians that suggested that a vast majority of us are eating too much and/or too much of the wrong thing. Maybe we should change our name to the True North Strong and Fat. Of course the cold climate, the ravages of chilling winds do tend to excite our appetites. It's no surprise that we love sweets and wolf down copious amounts of beer, fries, and donuts. Not only do they taste good on our half-frozen lips, they seem to keep us warmer. "Pass the gravy, please."

In the same documentary it was argued that our medical system was bearing the brunt of billions of dollars in bills associated with gluttony: heart disease and diabetes to mention only two such diseases. The cost of handling over-eating is certainly sinful if all we look at is the bottom line.

But here's the first issue about our common understanding of "sin." It all too often descends into a individual problem. As with gluttony, our ethical sensitivities focus on the person, and we picture an obese man stuffing his face with fried chicken and potato chips, grease dripping from his fingers. Or we imagine an over-sized woman who takes extra pieces of chocolate cake when no one is watching and squirrels away a bag of caramels in her desk drawer. But gluttony is not about individual behaviour, not initially.

At its roots, gluttony involves taking more than your share. If we recall the manna in the wilderness story of Exodus in which the people of God are fed each day by heavenly bread, we'll remember that in God's domain, people get only enough. Manna was available in the exact quantities necessary for each person's daily needs. You couldn't hoard it for a rainy day. There was no way to stockpile manna to sell to people who had missed their share. It wouldn't keep. By inference, the story is suggesting that food is not a commodity to be used for economic exploitation. It's sinful to take more than your share.

So when we hear about gluttony, particularly as a wealthy society, let's look well beyond the dilemma of over-eating. When, as a society, we take more than we require of the earth's resources and in that process rob others of their daily bread, we commit a grave injustice. Gluttony is not an eating disorder; it's an economic one.

Day 27:
Healing Touch

Opening Prayer
> *Move my hands to touch the wounded.*

Mark 5:41
> **And he [Jesus] takes the child by the hand....**

Healing is more than medicine and physical restoration. In the gospels it begins with touch.

Several years ago I was sick and in the hospital. Placed in a ward with three other patients, I discovered that the fellow to my right was in an especially bad way. I never discovered his disease, but it was quite disfiguring—not physically but socially. Whenever his tubes and bags were changed, the room was filled with a potent stench. All visitors cleared the ward when the nurses had to minister to this hapless guy. And you could see it in his eyes. It wasn't only the pain of the dis-ease that was killing him, the illness—that is to say the unpleasant smell, the sense of impurity, and the anti-social barriers that his bodily fluids imposed—the isolation and fear of contamination—that was the real illness, and it was harsh indeed. I could read between the lines of our conversation, that his self-worth was eroding rapidly. He was becoming an "untouchable."

During my stay, one astute nurse arrived one afternoon with a basin and a towel and for 15 minutes gave this very sick man a back rub and massage. I suppose it was written up in the charts as an hygienic necessity—towel bath or some such thing. What she actually did was not as important as the fact that she did it. She touched him. It made all the difference in the world. That was a real healing touch, because it said as no amount of verbal reassurance could, that this man while he was sick, perhaps dying, was still touchable.

May our table fellowship offer the same message.

Day 28:
The Sweet Bread of Life

Opening Prayer
> *Thank you, God, for all your sweetness, the delicious gifts of your table that remind us we are loved—without condition.*

Matthew 7:7–8
> **Ask—it'll be given to you; seek—you'll find; knock—it'll be opened for you. Rest assured: everyone who asks receives; everyone who seeks finds; and for the one who knocks it is opened.**

E-mail is a godsend to a writer in need of ideas. As the high season approaches, I pummel my wits looking for new ways to introduce the Holy Week themes—repentance, grief, guilt, redemption. Then up comes a message filled with Paschal one-liners focusing on the famous bunny that visits our homes leaving treats. Here's a selection of the better quips:

Walk softly and carry a big carrot! So true. I have always said that there is nothing like a well-placed bribe. For the workaholics pounding away at the office, here's some special advice: *All work and no play can make you a basket case.*

There were a few clever axioms for the weary: *Everyone is entitled to a bad hare day* or *Let happy thoughts multiply like rabbits.* As my mid-life drift continues in spite of my best exercising efforts, this line went down particularly well: *Some body parts should be floppy.*

But the best was the final quip: *The best things in life are still sweet and gooey.* You're thinking about the wrapped chocolate extravagances that grace your Easter table, nestled in straw. And while there is nothing like a good dose of glucose before dawn, I had a slightly more exalted meal in mind: sticky buns.

There is nothing like steaming Chelsea buns to accompany my hit of early morning caffeine. Hot, slathered in brown sugar syrup, giving off the heady scent of cinnamon, allspice, and ginger: Get out the butter and get out of my way. Say…let's pretend that just such a succulent delight is waiting on the plate in front of you. No one in sight to scold you or sour the taste. It's best eaten as finger food, so take a great bulging bite and then tell me there is no God.

Could we explain the joys of human invention apart from a benevolent Creator who wants us to indulge in the rich abundance of creation? As you chew on that imaginary sweet and gooey bread, what are you *not* thinking? I'll bet you're not thinking about cheating your neighbour. Do you have thoughts of malice towards your children? Not likely! In that instant when the sugar hits your taste buds, are you imagining what devious tricks you can play on your colleagues at the office? Neither jealousy nor greed, neither hate nor slander. As we enjoy the bounty of living, our hearts want to respond in kind. There's a warm glow that spreads over our bodies; we smile, moan with enchantment, lick our lips, and more than likely look around for someone with whom to share the moment if not also the sticky bun.

The human heart is hard wired like any circuit board and computer chip, programmed to respond in predictable patterns, and there is a direct link between gratification and gratitude. When we are graced with beauty or bounty, we quite naturally want to show our happiness by giving the same to others. Thanks giving is an automatic reflex—at least until a cynical and frightened world beats it out of us.

Think back to last year's Easter morning. Yes, of course there was a scramble for the eggs, but once they had their loot—what then? My son immediately wanted me to join him in devouring his stash. "Have some dad," he cooed, pulling me down to the kitchen floor. "Sit with me. There's so much good here."

Left on its own, the human heart wants to give, to share its joys with all those around. There's no need to preach justice or condemn gluttony. Just bring on the Chelsea buns and we will immediately understand—live out our love for others.

Sticky Buns

A great festive bread: Christmas or Easter morning fare.

1. Take 2 level tablespoons of dry yeast, 1 teaspoon of sugar, and ½ cup of warm water, and mix it together. Let it stand for 10 minutes.

2. Put 8 cups of white flour, ⅓ a cup each of sugar and olive oil, 1 tablespoon of salt in a bowl. Mix in 2½ cups of warm water. (2 eggs are optional.)

3. Once yeast is foamy, stir it into the flour mixture and start kneading.

4. Knead for 10 to 15 minutes. (If your dough is still stiff, add a tad more water; a touch more flour if it's still sticking to your hands.)

5. Roll it into a ball and plop it into a greased bread bowl. Then cover with a damp cloth.

6. Two hours later, tip it out onto a floured counter, roll it out into a rectangle 14 by 24 inches.

7. Cover the rectangle with syrup made as follows:

   a) Boil ½ cup butter or olive oil with 2 cups brown sugar, 1 cup white sugar, maple flavouring (optional), ½ cup water, 1 teaspoon cinnamon, 1 cup chopped nuts, 1 cup raisins.

   b) Spread evenly over the dough watching that the syrup doesn't drip off the sides.

8. Roll up the rectangle, trapping the syrup inside. Seal the final edge and slice the roll into inch-width rounds. Place rounds in a greased pan (having poured a little syrup on the bottom to cover it evenly).

9. Allow 2 to 2½ hours more to rise and bake them at 325°F for 30 to 35 minutes. (Temperature 325°–375°F, depending on your oven.)

10. Allow to cool and eat while still warm. If they sit for a day, slice thinly and cover in jam—works fine with grape jelly.

The Fourth Ingredient of Daily Bread Discipleship

Bread as The Great Leveller

The Fifth Sunday in Lent:
Don't Forget

Opening Prayer

> *God, may I never forget all your grace has given to me: life, laughter, love.*

Luke 24:25-27

> **And he [Jesus] said to them, "You people are so slow witted, so reluctant to trust everything the prophets have said! Was the Anointed One destined to undergo these things and enter into his glory?" Then starting with Moses and all the prophets, he interpreted for them every passage of scripture that referred to himself.**

Many years ago, my father visited a suburban nursing home as part of his duties as a young minister. It was a tightly run institution, so you can imagine his surprise when entering for his weekly rounds, he stepped into a swirling tempest. Everyone—nurses, doctors, patients, guests, orderlies—were dashing in and out of rooms. Every corridor was a chaotic jumble, a milling mob of confused patients and frustrated staff.

Dad is quick on the uptake and so he soon realized that a great search was in progress, a quest for false teeth. Not just one pair; everyone's dentures had disappeared. Some person or persons had crept around the previous night and removed all the teeth from the glass beside every bed. Alas, no one could gum down his or her breakfast and with dinner fast approaching, tensions and tempers were rising.

While my father was present neither the culprit nor the missing teeth were found, but eventually the riddle was solved. Under the mattress of one elder who, while she may have lost her memory, had lost neither her agility nor desire to collect things, was found a cache of uppers and lowers.

Now, most people don't label their false teeth, so how could anyone tell whose molars belonged to whom? In a community where forgetfulness is as common as the air they breathe, this was a vexing issue. Eventually, the administration held the dental version of hockey tryouts. All those without teeth came to a great, long table in search of their dentures. Over the course of several hours filled with "these don't feel right" and "here try mine" and "these are too sticky," all the uppers and lowers finally found a home.

But the story was not over. People weren't satisfied with their choices for in the time between theft and recovery gums had relaxed and grown soft, so no one's bite felt familiar. As the days went by, it was not uncommon for residents to continue the exchanging ritual—sometimes mid meal! There were even a few souls who went to their Maker swearing they had been robbed of their real bite.

While this is humorous, there is a tragic side to the loss of memory. Without some sense of where we have been, of our own stories, of what does and doesn't belong to us, we will blunder into old traps, unable to avoid the perilous pretence of the unseeing. Those who forget their history lack the humility of hindsight that must guide our daily path. Like the two walking on the road to Emmaus, we can fall prey to despair if we forget the promises of the old, old story. For adults, it is easy to get jaded about Lent—a ho-hum holiday. But think of it as a season for sustaining our collective memory, a chance to live our history again so that succeeding generations may come to know it by heart and recall what we might otherwise want to forget.

They need their teeth set right from the beginning.

Day 29:
Lowly Discipleship

Opening Prayer
> *God, the servant of all you love, bring me down to your level. Help my heart to see with lowly eyes; help my mind to delight in compassion; and help my hands to serve without boasting.*

John 13:15-16
> **"In other words, I've set an example: you are to do as I have done for you. I swear to God, slaves are never better than their masters; messengers are never superior to their senders."**

Come Holy Week, you may hear about foot washing—the lost sacrament. Often taking place during a Maundy Thursday evening liturgy, we would be wise to contemplate the meaning behind it before it happens.

First imagine what it must have been like in those times when dust, fungus, and contagion attacked the lower extremities of one's person. Foot washing was not the hygienic, sterile practice it might be today, as far from a professional pedicure as you can imagine. It's cruddy work, slopping off days of dirt with no deodorant, no anti-bacterial washes, and no latex gloves.

Today we're nervous about our feet. Mention a foot washing liturgy and you see people curl up their toes: "Not with my feet you don't." To expose your toes is risk taking. In the Palestinian world, feet were equally sensitive and never mentioned, not in polite company. Anyone who did important things didn't do feet. Foot washing, while necessary, was a vulgar job and it was left to women or slaves to perform. To get the bad taste that John implies, you'd probably have to compare it with wiping the toilet bowl. Think of those cleaners in the public washrooms scattered across this country. Someone has to clean them, but we don't advertise who, how or when, particularly at deeply spiritual moments.

If you are starting to feel uncomfortable, you're working your way into John's tale. Picture it, right at the apex of his story, when the trumpets are about to blare, announcing the entry of Emmanuel, God with us, in comes a guy with a toilet brush and slop bucket.

I find the foot-washing scene to be a marvellous contrast in John, the most theologically sophisticated of the gospels. In a text where the Christ is most god-like, most secure, John portrays him as the opposite. (One scholar once asked, "How do you crucify Jesus in John's gospel?" Answer: "Very carefully." The fourth evangelist makes it abundantly clear that this teacher from Nazareth knows he is God incarnate from the very beginning, no messing around with doubt or cries of dereliction on the cross.) This Great One, anointed as the coming Messiah, Son of the Most High, refuses to take the podium. He does not sit on a throne, but bends down to massage the wounds and hurts of his friends and followers.

Now we might be able to ignore this vision of the lowly Jesus—a biblical anomaly—had he not underlined his servanthood with a challenge to all who would be his disciples. John records his admonition, "In other words, I've set an example: you are to do as I've done for you." If you would be a disciple of this monarch, you must become as a servant—not taking on the high and mighty positions. The disciples of Jesus will be marked by their stooped shoulders, their willingness to serve one another, and by extension, the world.

The real Lord's Supper is a meal where no one is better or more important than another. Broken bread makes us one; all are servants, all are equal, and all are welcome.

Day 30:
No Spiritual Patronage

Opening Prayer
Do I have the courage to show you my feet—the vulnerable side of my soul? God, only you know me better than I do.

Mark 1:32-38a

In the evening at sundown, they would bring all the sick and demon-possessed to him. And the whole city would crowd around the door....And rising early, while it was still very dark, he went outside and stole away to an isolated place, where he started praying. Then Simon and those with him hunted him down. When they found him, they say to him, "They're all looking for you." But he replies, "Let's go somewhere else...."

Bread is more than bread. In the circle of Jesus it was an invitation to inner peace, the embodiment of God's abundance, a new economic order, and finally an inspiration for a new spiritual movement—one free of the assumptions of patronage.

In his text, *A Revolutionary Biography*, John Dominic Crossan maintains that this lowly, serving demeanour of the Jesus movement is a key to understanding the innovative nature of Christ's ministry. Jesus did not see himself as anyone's religious sugar daddy—the spiritual guru to whom the masses flocked. Quite the opposite, he was always correcting his followers and those who wanted to proclaim his grandeur. Look at Mark 1:21–39. It's the tale of the skyrocketing fame of the carpenter from Nazareth. He starts in Capernum—just your regular itinerant preacher. But no sooner is his first miracle out of the bag than thousands, "the whole city," it says, flocked to his door. You can picture the scene. The sick, blind, and lame are streaming to this new healer. Capernum

Chamber of Commerce has never seen so much traffic. Business is booming. This is the chance that every community would kill for.

Mark is building the scene carefully. You can feel the awe mount as Jesus heals the lost, casts out demons, and liberates those who are possessed. Jesus even heals the mother-in-law of one of his circle.

Now the audience who heard this first chapter would have a pretty good idea of what was coming next—just as we would. It's time to set up the tent and distribute the offering plates. The ministry needs administrative procedures and advance campaign coordinators.

The first impulse was and is to establishment, to setting up a pecking order and a patronage system. In first-century Palestine, these expectations were by no means secondary. It was a culture based on patronage. In that world, which had no real democratic or individualistic sensitivities, you couldn't reach anyone in the cast layers above your station without the good graces of a patron. And Mark's story has all the earmarks of the new patron being found in Galilee. Hallelujah! Jesus will be a messenger sent from God and to whom all the devout must turn if they want to reach the Almighty.

Except that Jesus won't play along. In verse 37, the disciples scurry up the hill after their leader and find him praying alone. They're pleased with Jesus, "They're all looking for you.... Come on, Jesus, it's time to start the show." But the Master replies, "Let's go somewhere else."

What? How can you have a legitimate religion, if you don't grow a church, if you don't establish your record and make people need you? Jesus was not interested in being handled, in having his followers hanging on his every action. I don't rely on Mark for this assumption. All of the gospels show that Jesus is an itinerant, the man who never settles down. When the rabbi sends out his followers in Luke 10, the message is clear. You're not about building a church or a club. You are to take no security, no pension plan or RRSP. The Jesus followers will be known by their radical trust in the community they enter. Grace is not owned, nor stored up, nor located in a specific sacred space. The holy comes to earth in the flash of spontaneous encounters and in the exchange of hospitality and healing.

A Jewish parable states it well: "If you would see God, you must bend down very low."

Day 31:
Growing Up

Opening Prayer

> *God, there are times when I am alone—my friends, family, even you desert me. The old, old story seems empty, and my nursery rhyme prayers go nowhere. Lift me, help me stand, help me know I am yours.*

Mark 15:34

> **And at three o'clock in the afternoon, Jesus shouted at the top of his voice: "*Eloi, Eloi, lema sabachthani?*" ("My God, My God, why did you abandon me?")**

The Christ we have fixed in our stained glass imaginations is usually surreal and sublime—head and shoulders above anxiety and consequently quite unhelpful. The Jesus we meet in scriptures has his feet planted firmly in the ambiguity of human existence. He embraced the doubters as friends. He welcomed agnostics and seekers. He himself doubted his own mission when he tasted abandonment on the cross.

It is no surprise then that one of the key notes in his ministry was his invitation for the spiritually smug to risk their "blessed assurance" and admit a few misgivings about their own virtue. It wasn't that Jesus wanted to destroy faith. On the contrary, he came to restore it. But he knew, as many Christian movements have subsequently forgotten, that God's rule on earth will not come as any of us suspect.

Let's back up. If we proclaim that Jesus is, as the creeds claim, one with God, then we must recognize that the gospel describes Christ's divine connection in unexpected ways. The God who comes to earth is met among the outcasts and hidden in the shame and agony of crucifixion. The God revealed in Jesus is, as Martin Luther suggested, a "Hidden God, a *Deus Obsconditus.*" Jesus is not a predictably triumphal, warrior-like deity, but hidden in the opposite, a lowly servant to all. The divinity, which we so loudly proclaim at Easter, is hidden, altered, not at all patterned after the monarchical template some might fashion for their KING Jesus. It is a divinity that can be known only through suffering. God is known in God's opposite—not seen by the masters at the table, but only by the servants who clear the table and wash the feet.

The church resisted this theological understanding—it was too demanding, confounding our neat categories. We used the image of servant discipleship as one among many incentives for disciples to remain childish in their faith. In past ages, we have proposed that people not trouble themselves with deep questions. "Just believe." We encouraged a "Jesus loves me this I know" approach to soul work. Lay people were amateurs and they needed a professional to receive the gifts of the spirit—a curious twist in ecclesiastical practice since Jesus himself refused to be that kind of religious broker.

His bread was more than bread. It was a call to grow up; to cease using religion as a crutch and to think your way into your apprehensions and suffering—it is there God will be found.

Day 32:
Drop Your Guilt and Walk

Opening Prayer
> *God, get my guilt! Take my self-loathing away. Ask me to rise up and walk in maturity and health.*

John 5:2-6
> **In Jerusalem, by the Sheep [Gate], there is a pool, called *Bethzatha* in Hebrew. It has five colonnades, among which numerous invalids were usually lying around....[They were waiting for some movement of the water. Remember, a heavenly messenger would descend into the pool from time to time and agitate the water. When that happened the first one into the pool would be cured of whatever disease he or she had.] One man had been crippled for 38 years. Jesus observed him realizing he had been there a long time. "Do you want to get well?" he asks him.**

Look in the bathroom mirror and what do your see? I guarantee that whatever else you might notice, when you study yourself closely you see a guilt victim. Human beings may be hard wired to love, but we are also a defenceless species when it comes to the spread of culpability.

Guilt happens (especially during Lent). There's no use pointing fingers—"It was my mother's church moralisms" or "my father's strict code"—guilt is a free-floating virus that can attach itself to almost every human activity: wild parties while mom and dad are out, sitting alone in a dark room, staying out too late, coming home too early. Your racial or religious background is largely irrelevant. Cultures choose different objects or actions on which to attach shame, but no one escapes.

Guilt rules! Guilt is often associated with marital discord. There's nothing like separation and divorce to lower your defences. Walking down the street, you picture again the faces of your children as they "heard the news" and you want to melt into the cracks in the sidewalk. They didn't ask for the break-up. Adults may be in control of the decision—painful though it may be. Kids are helpless, and you whip your self-esteem for causing them pain, and yet you can't turn back.

"Why," you ask, "Would people wallow in guilt? Why wouldn't they want to be whole?" Three reasons. First, it masks the pain of emptiness. Better to feel something rather than nothing. Second, it's easier to be a victim—isn't that the point of the story from John concerning the lame at the side of the pool of *Bethzatha*? Even self-inflicted injury takes less energy and looks safer than emotional responsibility. Third, guilt is a cheap psychology trick. We pay the penalty of bad feelings so we can keep doing what we think we shouldn't do.

Guilt traps. Getting better takes courage. (The crippled man in John's gospel above proves the point.) Healthy people can only stomach this level of self-loathing for short periods of time before they want relief.

The first step in getting the guilt monkey off your back is to admit you've got the bug. There's nothing more pathetic than dog-eared souls who, when asked, claim, "Oh, no, I don't feel guilty." If you're flesh and blood you're going to feel culpable when your primary relationship hits a roadblock. So recite it like a mantra: "I feel guilty." It's hard to repeat because it's an acknowledgement that we are not what we want to be: perfect, free of blemishes, and our own masters. Facing the burdened state of your soul is a step in the right direction because when we unmask the beast of guilt, we can better determine which actions are attempts to cover up or feed it.

But there's another step. You have to tell someone. Go to a close friend (this will test their loyalty) or you may choose to pay a professional. In any case, it's time to spill the beans. Guilt will not disappear until you lay out your dark side for someone to inspect and it may take more than one session.

Guilt costs. There's a reason why priests say that confession is good for the soul. You will discover, first, that you are not alone. Every Adam and Eve screws up. And second, that there is a miracle called absolution. It is indeed unthinkable but true, that those who know us best (broken and bent though we may be) love us most. You may think that this absolution is the get-out-of-guilt-free ticket. It's not. Rather, it is the affirmation that you are a dearly loved child of the earth. Nothing you do can alter that state. Even your atheism and scorn are not obstacles to the fact that the One who made this Universe loves you!

No matter your theology, when you stare into that mirror, know that you are not defined by your errors. Admit the guilt, name your faults and feelings, share them, own them, and let them go. Now get out of the washroom and start living this new day.

Guilt free.

Day 33:
The Special Bread

Opening Prayer
> *Free me from my piety, O God. Loosen my prayers—pry them away from cloying self-interest. Drag my heart away from egotism. Set a right spirit within me—one open to joy as equally as to sorrow.*

Matthew 6:16-18
> **When you fast, don't make a spectacle of your remorse as the pretenders do. As you know, they make their faces unrecognizable so their fasting may be publicly recognized....Comb your hair and wash your face, so your fasting may go unrecognized in public.**

There are a number of theories regarding the origins of the flaky bread we call croissants. Some suggest it was an inventive European attempt to appease invading armies of Saracen soldiers during the late Middle Ages, its shape, a moon or half circle, commemorating their Sultan's symbol.

I prefer to think of the croissant as an antidote against perverted Lenten piety. Past generations have tormented the flesh in the belief that this is what God desired—no eggs, no butter, no joy. But Matthew argues against these shows of spiritual hubris advising that when we are fasting, let it not show; our devotion to God should be understated and not used for self-aggrandisement. So Lenten admonitions against rejoicing leave me cold. Rather, as the pain of Calvary draws closer, should we not rejoice in the delicacy and frailty of God's creation? A few warm croissants at this stage in our journey toward Easter are just the ticket.

Croissants (An Excuse to Eat Butter)

It took me many attempts to get this bread to work as described, and you too may find it unduly demanding. My advice...enjoy...the worst that can happen is that you'll end up with a very rich buttery bread. The best...well there is no better communion bread. A hint...watch the rolling and keep the dough cold so the butter doesn't melt. You want it to stay cold so that each time you roll it out you create more layers of butter and dough.

1. Heat ⅞ cup warm milk until scalded.

2. Mix in 1 tablespoon olive oil, 1½ tablespoons sugar, 1 teaspoon of salt. Allow mixture to cool to warm.

3. While the above cools, take 1 level tablespoon of dry yeast, 1 teaspoon of sugar, and ⅓ cup of warm water, and mix it together. Let it stand for 10 minutes and then add it to the cooled milk.

4. Stir in 2½ to 3½ cups of white flour—enough to make a good spongy dough.

5. Knead for 10 to 15 minutes. (If your dough is still stiff, add a tad more water; a touch more flour if it's still sticking to your hands.)

6. Roll it into a ball and plop it into a greased bread bowl. Then cover with a damp cloth.

7. 1½ hours later, tip it out onto a floured counter.

8. Roll out the dough into a rectangle ¼ inch thick and 12 by 20 inches.

9. Take a cup of cold butter and knead it under cold water until it is soft (the point is to get a soft dough that is still cold).

10. Spread the cold, soft butter over ⅔ of the dough. Fold the unbuttered ⅓ onto ⅓ of the buttered dough and then lift the final ⅓ on top.

11. Roll this dough out into a rectangle ¼ inch thick and then fold as in step #10.

12. Roll it out for a third time into a rectangle ¼ inch thick and then fold again.

13. Place dough in the fridge for 1 hour.

14. Roll the dough out again 3 times—folding as above each time and then place in the fridge to chill for another hour.

15. Roll out the dough one last time, cut into 6 inch squares, and cut each square in the diagonal until you have the rolled dough dissected into triangles.

16. Begin at the wide end of each triangle to roll into the croissant shape.

17. Place on a greased cookie sheet—chill for ½ hour and then bake immediately at 400°F for 10 minutes and then reduce the heat to 350°F for another 10 to 15 minutes.

There's no question that this recipe takes practice. Again, watch that you don't allow the butter too much into the dough—overly zealous rolling can do it. The point is to create multiple thin layers of butter and dough—it gives this bread its flaky, subtle flavour. Get out the jam and brie cheese, then invite over the neighbours. This bread is best eaten once it has cooled from the oven.

Day 34:
Night Vision: Preparing for the Palm Branches

Opening Prayer

> *I never think of tomorrow. Today is sufficient for my soul. Thank God that I can't see what will happen around the corner.*

Luke 19:29–30

> **And it so happened as he [Jesus] got close to Bethphage and Bethany at the mountain called Olives, that he sent off two of the disciples with these instructions: "Go into the village across the way. As you enter it, you will find a colt tied there, one that has never been ridden. Untie it and bring it here."**

Until recently night vision capabilities were reserved for armed forces. No longer. You can now order a specially equipped Cadillac with eyes that see three times as far down the highway as before. This innovation can detect potential danger 400-500 yards away.

Think of the possibilities. The deer that darts from the bushes will be seen between 12 to 18 seconds before a potential collision. The lost motorists flagging down your car, asking for help, pose no threat—plenty of time to make a judgment call on their sincerity! In an image similar to that of a photo negative, the child running onto the road or the moose staring down the traffic will be visible—dancing just above the hood of the car.

While the cost is still relatively high, $2,000, the savings in life and limb could prove to be remarkable. While only a quarter of our driving time is spent at night, half the traffic fatalities on the roads happen after dark. Besides, a scant 10 years ago this night vision would have cost hundreds of thousands of dollars, and so a couple of grand is a bargain.

The system works on heat rather than light. A forward-looking infrared scanner reads and measures variables in temperature. It can detect a differential as low as 0.3 of a degree. So, for example, if you pointed your Seville at a tree you would be able to detect the loss of heat from the central trunk as it escapes through the small twigs at the end of branches. A dubious advantage unless you're a botanist, but you will catch the pulsing signal from the exhaust of a car that is hidden from view and presumably avoid perilous proximity.

Tomorrow many believers will be celebrating the triumphal entry into Jerusalem by Jesus. You know the tale. Calling attention to an ancient tradition that the chosen one of God would arrive in the holy city on a donkey, the rabbi from Galilee is met by festive crowds who herald his approach by breaking palms from the trees by the path, waving them frantically and strewing the road with coats. Hallelujah!

Now imagine if the humble colt on which Christ sat had been equipped with Detroit's latest gimmick. Maybe he could have seen with clarity that there was a cross waiting at the end of his road. No more uncertainty, the mystery would have been revealed with stark terror and Jesus could have steered clear. But this is foolishness, according to Christian dogma. Christ embraced the humiliation and pain of crucifixion precisely because it was in that act that God was revealed in a unique way to the world. No cross. No Emmanuel. No God with us.

Jesus didn't need infrared indicators to see the dangers on his journey. Everyone knew full well that those who attacked the sacred symbols of spiritual and political power were in for a rough ride. The irony is that the Christian tradition has gone out of its way to provide religious infrared systems to its believers. For hundreds of years disciples have been told not to focus on the cross, but to watch the flickering images further down the road! It is the triumph of the empty tomb that should hold our attention. Alas, this long-sightedness robs the believer of an essential ignorance. It is the assurance of our faith that undermines our faith. Because we already know what is going to happen and how the tale will end, the immanent and subversive dimension of the Jesus event is lost to us. We lose sight of the fact that early believers saw God as a Hidden Being and so we don't have to struggle with our anxieties and doubts—the fountain head of all true belief!

Let us remember that the cross was not a noble instrument. It was a tool of annihilation inflicting not just a tortuous death, but promising by its very nature that you would be wiped out as a dignified child of the Creator. When it had done its work, you would be shredded and torn.

The modern Christian's problem is that we are not troubled by this contradiction. We see too well and therefore we see nothing. This Palm Sunday, we could ask for no better gift than being struck with night blindness—only in groping about in the dark for a time do we come to know the God who emerges in the twilight of our fears.

$\mathcal{H}$oly Week

Stories for the Journey

Palm Sunday:
Pinch the Sparkle

Opening Prayer

> *God, help me to know joy when I find it—to see it as one of your greatest miracles. These moments are a gift...may I always live them fully.*

Luke 19:35-37

So they brought it [the colt] to Jesus. They threw their cloaks on the colt and helped Jesus to mount it. And as he rode along, people would spread their cloaks on the road. As he approached the slope of the Mountain of Olives, the entire throng of disciples began to cheer and shout praise to God for all the miracles they had seen.

Years ago, my father's family owned a small cottage by Lake Huron. Given the rudimentary styles of holiday practices in those days, "shack" or "hut" would be a better translation. Each summer Saturday my Uncle Jack and Aunt Edna would travel to the beach for sun and sand. Jack never stayed overnight, making the round trip twice each weekend while Edna would preside over the family court that built up around her.

My Aunt had two prized possessions, a parrot that could utter greetings to all visitors to the house (Jack taught it to swear) and her diamond ring. The latter was a gift from Jack. The central stone was magnificent. In a household where the weekly rent became a matter of daily concern, the diamond stood out. As bright as it was extravagant, it might have been a mocking contrast to the poverty of Jack and Edna's lifestyle if it had not been so beautiful.

On one fateful July night, when Edna was strolling the beach alone, the diamond slipped from its moorings and fell into the sand. Jack had already left for the day, and the children were in bed. Search as she might, it was a hopeless cause. The treasure was lost, and Edna was numb with shock. Her heirloom was gone and not even the application of several liberal drinks from her summertime neighbours could revive her spirits.

For the next few weekends the subject of the lost diamond was the focus of lake-side debates. Where had it gone? How long would it take to be ground into powder? Who might recover it in another age?

On the last Sunday of August, with the cottage almost boarded up for the summer, Jack went for a stroll down by the water. "Just to clear my head before the drive home." The moon was out, and its rays glanced off the crystalline edges of beach sand and sent a shower of sparks across the water. He watched this concert of light with delight and noticed how one particular sparkle was brighter and more persistent than the rest. Even as he stood nearby, its fire did not fade. Bending down, Jack pinched the sparkle and, miracle of miracles, came up with Edna's diamond. An impossible possibility!

Joy is as fleeting. It is not a certainty. It comes with no guarantee. It is as predictable as finding a diamond in the sand. And yet in spite of the growing storm clouds, the disciples found the courage to rejoice. Palm Sunday is a brief moment of celebration before the dark passions of Holy Week. People sang and rejoiced in all the marvels of their Maker. The crowd-waving frenzy is a small spark in the midst of deepening darkness. Like all instances of happiness, the trick is to enjoy it now. Don't wait for something better. Don't ask about the probabilities and practicalities. Pinch the sparkle when you see it—who knows what miracles will be waiting for you when you do.

Day 35:
When You Think You're a Failure

Opening Prayer

> *There are days, months sometimes, when I think I am failure. God,*
> *you know it. I wallow around in my misdemeanors and never look*
> *up. Save me!*

Matthew 7:9-11

Who among you would hand a son a stone when it's
bread he's asking for?...So if you, shiftless as you are,
know how to give your children good gifts, isn't it much
more likely that your father in the heavens will give good
things to those who ask him?

When was the last time you sang "Gentle Nettie Moore"? Then there's, "The Little White Cottage," a classic for fireside sing-a-longs. And if you're in a militant mood, who doesn't hum "We Conquer or Die"? What? You haven't heard of these tunes? Neither had I until recently.

As I sat down to write my weekly article on faith, I was feeling like a failure. Perhaps this has happened to you. No matter how well you construct them, your words sag and crisp ideas go limp. Some people call it writer's block, but from my perspective it looked a lot like the festive futility. Easter is the scourge of all preachers and columnists—what to say that is new and refreshing? Along with Christmas it is the pivotal moment in our emotional calendars—a day that brings to consciousness all the blemishes and burdens we have stored away in our mental sub-basement. Rather than dwelling on the light, our minds cotton onto the dark side. So as the last week of Lent rears its head, you start rehearsing your errors: the many earnest e-mails you ignored or the gruff words you uttered. Deeper down you discover the heavy-weights. The fight with your sister comes to mind and that brings up the bent feelings that still exist between you and your mom, feelings that seem never to get straightened out for very long. And while you're on the subject of how low you can go, why did you ignore the hand of friendship extended by an old school chum? Moving on to other fertile ground, you sniff out your misdemeanours at the office and relive the mismanaged portfolio and the lost report. And don't forget the indignities you inflicted on others. Failure. There are times when you think it's written on your forehead in indelible ink.

James Pierpont, the composer of those pieces mentioned above was, to all intents and purposes, a failure. Pierpont was a nineteenth-century dry goods merchant whose only musical platform was to be the choir director of his father's church in Savannah, Georgia. But he was also the author of a song that every North American knows, sings, and loves: "Jingles Bells."

Pierpont had a remarkably uneventful career—serving in the Civil War with the Confederate Cavalry, selling paint and varnish to make a living, dying a forgotten man. His name is rarely found in encyclopaedias—even those of musical composers list him only in passing as the uncle of a more noteworthy, wealthy financier. A failure. And yet from that humble abode came a glorious tune.

Okay, "Jingle Bells" doesn't mention Jesus or the Virgin Mary, or Joseph. And yes, it has been co-opted by secular commercial interests as the best way to sell everything from yo-yo's to yogurt. But don't think of the jingles or how they are used. Picture instead the circle of smiles that is born when we chant that old tune. Can you see the joy come to earth? For those few minutes as we speak of activities that few have ever experienced (when was the last time you took a ride in a one-horse, open sleigh?), we forget our worries and woes and remember that happiness is possible in spite of our failures.

Outwardly, Pierpont might look like a dud, but to bring such a sense of well-being to millions as they turn to his song for solace and sunrise is no failure. Neither are you.

Worth is not measured by fame or fortune, but by shared laughter. So join with me! (Who cares if it's a Christmas tune? It speaks about untarnished joy—an Easter theme for sure.) "Jingle bells, jingle bells, jingle all the way. Oh what fun...."

Day 36:
The Universal "I'm Sorry" Day

Opening Prayer

There are times when I regret what I have done, when I curse myself for what I have not done. God, help me. Give me a second chance, to make it better, to say I'm sorry. I promise I won't waste the opportunity.

Matthew 5:48

To sum up, you are to be unstinting in your generosity in the way your heavenly Father's generosity is unstinting.

HEAR YE! HEAR YE!
LET THERE BE AN INTERNATIONAL DAY DEVOTED TO APOLOGIES.
In response to popular demand, I declare on behalf of all the world's religions that there shall be a day given over to the act of contrition. This holy day shall be celebrated around the globe on the same date. All people, no matter their race, creed, nationality or gender shall use this time to seek out those they have wronged and express their regret and remorse.

Do you think it would work? It has all the earmarks of an idea long overdue. The human heart is burdened with untold guilt. Silly insults of childhood proportions still rankle in our souls, and those adult size betrayals—well, we all have them. So why not have a special occasion when the slate could be wiped clean?

For the reluctant, the Universal "I'm Sorry" Day would be a stimulus, for the bold it would be justification. The aggrieved would no longer be plagued by doubt—they'd know when they were going to get their just deserts. And the heartless would have no excuse. At least once a year they'd have an opportunity to change their ways. Timidity would be banished and truculence would be wiped out.

Given the pain and difficulty of apologizing, making it an international festival would surely remove some of the stigma. It would no longer be an obligation so much as a party game. Besides, we'd all get better with practice, and in time and given the natural human impulse to virtue, we'd find creative and meaningful ways to make the words "I'm sorry" both magical and meaningful. Of course, each faith tradition would devise a means for giving such a celebration its own particular coloring, but I can imagine that nations would also want to confer a secular flavour on such a unique carnival. Italians would say, "I'm sorry" with passion and pasta perhaps, while the French would use roses and red wine. The British would do it standing stock still, Latinos would dance their sorries, and Canadians would find a way to apologize on ice.

And there's no question that the multinational giants would leap on such a chance to advertise their products. Can you picture it? Selling pop and apologies. No doubt, someone would invent a universally accepted flower that says, "I'm sorry" and we'd soon be sending it to each other by the dozens. Who cares if the NASDAQ is falling, the Universal "I'm Sorry" Day will do what monetary policies can't.

In a quirky way it does make sense. If our society can establish special weeks to remember the victims of cancer, or months dedicated to celebrate amateur sports, or years devoted to the protection of children, why not a single day for the soul? If there is anything that needs to be elevated above the mundane and given a loftier profile, it is the act of saying "sorry." We've been subjected to so many apologizing politicians lately, that the act of saying "I'm sorry" has become all too commonplace and, dare I say it, empty. Is there anyone out there who is still "touched" by the tears?

Apologies, on their own, solve nothing—nice to hear, but useless unless they are accompanied by evidence of true contrition, the re-establishment of just relations, and commitment to live a new life. In that case, to be real, an apology is almost the last word that is offered, not the first. It's a strenuous, demanding task. Perhaps the declaration of a Universal "I'm Sorry" Day should come with a disclaimer: "For mature adults only. Not to be left in the hands of minors."

Day 37:
Planting Instruments: Memories and Laughter

Opening Prayer
> *Creator of Universe, help me never to forget the touch of your hand,*
> *the warmth of your embrace, and the smile of your grace.*

Luke 22:19
> **And he took a loaf, gave thanks, broke it into pieces,**
> **offered it to them, and said, "This is my body which is**
> **offered for you. Do this as my memorial."**

A dibber is a Maritime garden tool. Looking like a pastry rolling pin with the southern end whittled down to a point, it is used to plant beans and other large seed vegetables. Much like the ancient field stick, a dibber is ideal for punching the perfect hole into the tilled earth, providing a homey spot for every seed and a single seed for every hole.

I want to thank the close friends who gave my dibber to me—not because I have a green thumb or an inclination to start a bean field business, but because it reminds me of the extent to which some people will go in order to hold back the chaos. Whereas most folks scatter their seeds in a hastily dug row of dirt, sprinkle down some water, and pray for the best, the dibber digger is precise.

But I also keep the dibber close at hand because of a totally unrelated matter. It reminds me of another hole-making practice still employed in my New Brunswick home town: grave digging. Those of us who live in small, isolated villages know what I mean. If there is no funeral director living nearby, a gang of men gather at the cemetery out behind the church and dig—three yards long, forty-two inches across, and six feet down. It's not just that the community doesn't want to refit the gate to allow a back-hoe into the graveyard. The rite of grave digging is an opportunity for showing respect and honor to the deceased, drawing a line of order through the chaos of death. Can a machine feel anything for the elders who go before us? Human hands are needed to lay our loved ones to rest.

Last week in Riley Brook, a 94-year-old matron passed on, and the grave digging is set for 7:30 a.m. This small community isn't blessed with a Tim Horton's, so Bill and Bob bring several thermoses for the 15 men who walk through the fog to the designated spot. (Don't weep for them. What Bill and Bob add to their coffee you can't get at your local java joint.)

The gravesite is marked off, and everyone takes turns at the shovelling. While a few handle the spades, the remainder are required to recite stories—some relating to the departed soul, but many just funny tales of local color. There was the time Uncle Jake was found grovelling around the dump looking for a gift for his wife. Talk about cheap! Or how about the night Hester's dress fell off at the Christmas dance. Then there's Ned who never met a river rapid he couldn't maneuver with a pole in one hand and a pipe in the other. And Gary who hasn't had a hunting license in four years, but every year calls at least one moose out into the clearing down by the brook. Feats of courage and cowardice, acts of kindness and cruelty—they all get shared at the graveside. This is life and death.

The humor is entirely appropriate. Apart from easing the grief we feel, laughter is the chief antidote to our fear of dying and the best way to honor those who have been taken from our circle; for in chuckles and guffaws, we remind ourselves that the here and now is all we are given. Enjoy and cherish the beauty in each passing day and you know the secret of dying well. One of the essential food groups for these last days of Lent is the combination of memory and laughter.

Like my dibber, grave digging is a precision instrument. But in this latter case, it's not about the size or shape of the hole, but how well the tool suits the need. "So pass me that shovel and tell me again how Jake shopped at the town dump for all his presents."

Day 38, Maundy Thursday:
Servanthood: Who Does Feet?

Opening Prayer

> *God, give me the bread that satisfies my over-reaching piety. Help me to be content with me—not a saint, not a sinner, just fully human.*

John 13:12-14

> **When he had washed their feet, he put his clothes back on and sat down at the table again. "Do you realize what I've done?" He asked. "You call me your master, and you're right: that's who I am. So if I am your master and teacher and have washed your feet, you ought to wash each other's feet."**

A brochure that came across my desk in this Lenten season was advertising the "Sixth Annual Gospel Extravaganza" titled: "Loving According to John—an eyewitness account of the Easter story as told by John the Apostle."

I'm generally sympathetic to such dramatic presentations—restoring a subversive bite to the gospel—but the advertising for this particular dramatic portrayal of the fourth evangelist's story struck me as curious, because in the glossy theatre shot featured on the posters and in the flyers, they pictured Jesus at the table—elevating the bread as part of the Lord's Supper.

Now at a glance, that seems entirely appropriate. The Lord's Supper is after all the central meal of the good news, the vehicle of God's grace and most likely the original model for the gatherings of the Jesus movement, except that John's gospel contains no communion. Right when you expect to hear the words of consecration, "This is my body broken for you...Do this in remembrance of me," instead of the evocative image of the sacrificial lamb, the martyr of blood and bread, John's Jesus insists on taking the role of slave. Rather than being master of the feast, the rabbi from Galilee wraps a towel around his waist and wipes people's feet—the menial and degrading work of the lowest in that world.

It's a simple, but dramatic picture. Jesus uses his table fellowship to portray a new model of piety—no priestly ministrations, no magical piety, no spiritual patrons. His circle will be characterized by servanthood, not grandeur.

On this holy day, why don't we join in? We'll get our socks off and spend the day thinking about what will happen when he gets to us.

Day 39, Good Friday:
The Bread for the Shadow. Who Killed Jesus?

Opening Prayer
> *God, help me. Sustain me through the long night.*

Matthew 27:22
> **Pilate says to them, "What should I do with Jesus known as 'the Anointed'?" Everyone responded, "Have him crucified!"**

We crucified our Maker—the basic message of Good Friday. We took the gift of love and trampled it into the ground. We were frightened, more than a bit intimidated, and jealous…we let our envy have full reign. We nailed God's purpose to a cross. It was a dark hour that all our excuses can't wipe out.

While we wait through this shadow time, let's get our hands busy with a bread for this day: hot cross buns.

Hot Cross Buns

1. Take 2 level tablespoons of dry yeast, 1 teaspoon of sugar, and ½ cup of warm water, and mix it together. Let it stand for 10 minutes.
2. Put 8 cups of white flour, ⅓ cup of brown sugar, 1 teaspoon each of cinnamon, allspice, and ginger, and 1 tablespoon of salt into a bowl.
3. Add the mixed candied fruit (2 cups) and the raisins (1½ cups)—the amounts can vary, depending on your taste.
4. Mix in 1½ cups of warm water and 1 cup warm milk, and add 3 beaten eggs.

5. Once yeast is foamy, stir it into the flour mixture, and start kneading.

6. Knead for 10 to 15 minutes. (If your dough is still stiff, add a tad more water; a touch more flour if it's still sticking to your hands.) You'll have fun scooping up all the raisins and candied fruit pieces that fall out of the dough as you do the kneading.

7. Roll it into a ball and plop it into a greased bread bowl. Then cover with a damp cloth.

8. Two hours later, tip it out onto a floured counter and shape into 20–24 small balls. Flatten each one so that it looks like a miniature of the traditional hot cross bun shape. Place on a greased cookie sheet.

9. Beat an egg white and brush each bun so that it is well coated. Then cut a cross in the top of each bun.

10. Allow 2–2½ hours more to rise and bake them at 350°F for 25–25 minutes. (Temperature 325°–375°F, depending on your oven.)

11. (Optional) When the buns have cooled, add a line of white icing in the cross that was cut into the top.

The recipe can be adapted in two ways: (1) Change the shape of the dough after the first rising—turn it into three loaves of sweet bread—let rise 2 hours and bake for 40 minutes. (2) Use this recipe to make bagels—after the first rising, shape into 24 balls, pinch hole in the middle, "boil" the bagels according to the traditional bagel method—hot water bath 3½ minutes per side—and bake for 25 minutes at 350°F.

Day 40, Holy Saturday:
A Hint of Flowers

Opening Prayer
> *I hate to wait. I hate to wait. I hate to wait. God of the waiters, stay with me in the in-between times of my life.*

Luke 24:9-11
> **And returning from the tomb, they related everything to the eleven and to everybody else. The group included Mary of Magdala and Joanna and Mary the mother of James, and the rest of the women companions. They related their story to the apostles, but their story seemed nonsense to them, so they refused to believe the women.**

In the in-between time, it is hard to keep believing. Miracles can't be scheduled; the plausible seems to overpower the impossible all too easily. After the Good Friday nightmare, this despair had overtaken the followers of Jesus. As they sat through their first Holy Saturday, the finality of the Golgotha overshadowed them. All was darkness, and no glimmer of hope was visible. The grave had won!

In the heart of the city of Paris there is a famous cemetery, Cemetaire Pere LaChaise. It's like a "Who's Who" of nobility and celebrity, containing many superb sculptures and carvings, testimonies written in granite to their owners' importance. Heloise and Abelard—the great lovers of the Middle Ages—are found here. A twentieth-century superstar, Jim Morrison, is also buried in Pere LaChaise. Edith Piaff and Oscar Wilde are lying nearby.

Crowded in a side street of tombstones, there is an elegant statue of a delicate woman bending over in mourning, arms outstretched, a picture of grief, and on the pedestal, the simple words, "Fred Chopin." The great romantic composer rests in resounding understatement. On the surface his tomb smells of death and decay. Mould creeps up the stones of the walkway, declaring that the grave has won—no one rises from this place.

But...in spite of the finality, the impossibility of new life, there is a miracle that happens every day at Chopin's grave. Without organization or intention, a dozen roses appear in the arms of the marble woman bending over his remains. Sometimes several bunches of flowers grace his tomb. A small victory, yes. But a miracle nonetheless.

Is there a more fitting metaphor for the Easter celebration of Christians than the re-awakening of the flowers of nature? The Holy Day wasn't planned for this reason—not entirely. Established in conjunction with the Jewish festival of Passover, Easter happens on the Sunday closest to the 14th day of Nisan, a month in the Hebraic calendar. Palestine, while closer to the equator, does experience a blossoming of the land. While the Jewish festival is essentially a recounting of God's salvation of the people of Israel, there is a similar thread linking the eternal world and its weather patterns and the interior journey of the soul.

Whether speaking of Passover or Easter, our spirits are longing for the message that only a glowing clutch of roses can speak: "Death is not the final word." Play on, Chopin!

Easter Sunday:
Walking off the Biblical Map

Opening Prayer

> *Sometimes I try too hard to finish my own story, control the dia-*
> *logue, tie up the loose ends, and finish the plot. God, keep me open,*
> *allowing your mystery to unfold of its own accord.*

Mark 16:8

> **And once they [Mary of Magdala and Mary the mother**
> **of James and Salome] got outside, they ran from the**
> **tomb, because great fear and excitement got the better**
> **of them. They didn't breathe a word of it to anyone: talk**
> **about terrified!**

Without the assistance of positioning satellites and accurate measuring instruments, speculation and careful guessing were the chief tools of the early cartographers. Given their low-tech methods, the results were remarkable. Nevertheless, there were many unknowns beyond the edges of the civilized world. And so to embellish their ignorance, monsters, dragons, and serpents were featured around the parameters of these early maps as if to say: beyond this point, only demons dwell.

The legend goes that a particularly ambitious and fastidious Roman commander had led his legion to the frontiers of the Empire and beyond. In hostile, foreign country, he sent back an urgent message that read: "Have marched off the map, please send directions." I often think of that Imperial leader in this Easter season of the Christian church, that time when we declare with bravado that Christ is risen. We're walking off certain ground and entering the land where myth grows.

If we accept the scholarly consensus that Mark's gospel was written first of the four gospels and that the other evangelists followed his narrative pattern, the empty tomb represents the edge of the Christian map. Prior to Easter morning, Matthew, Luke, and John follow the familiar route laid out by Mark. The Jesus story begins at a baptism, proceeds to the wilderness, and then returns to Galilee where the healing and feeding ministry takes place. After Peter's declaration that Jesus is the anointed one of God, the scene shifts to Jericho and then Jerusalem. Confrontations on the temple mount lead to an upper room betrayal, the garden of tears, trials, and crucifixion.

But once Good Friday has passed, we enter resurrection land where Mark's plot ends at an empty tomb. At this point the other three gospels ride off in all directions. Matthew features the great ascension commissioning, "Go out into the world, baptizing all peoples." Luke has the intriguing story of the road to Emmaus apparition when two disciples don't recognize their Lord until he breaks bread with them. And John takes the merry company of Christ back to their fishing nets and a seaside picnic. Here Jesus commissions Peter to, "Feed my sheep." The lack of pattern in the Easter appearances of Jesus reveals a very significant conundrum. What does the Christian believer make of the resurrection?

Mark seems to indicate that the mystery of the risen Christ is best left alone. Rather, he leaves us with the women and their fear. It wasn't that they were frightened for their lives. They were fearful of life, what this miraculous gift might cost and how Emmanuel, "God with us," might change all dreams and hopes.

Matthew, as the church gospel, uses the resurrection to solidify the institutional claims of Christianity. He was writing for a fledging religion trying to find its spiritual feet. Jesus rose from the dead and therefore proves the validity of the Christ cult.

In typical fashion, Luke underlines the central theme of his narrative: God is not known easily and certainly not by those who think they should know better. God appears *incognito*. Just when you think you have him in sight, there she isn't. A tricky gospel and my favorite.

Alas, John can't resist the splashy finish. Jesus will not go from this earth without clear evidence that he is indeed a resurrected body/spirit. His instructions to the future church "fathers" are explicit: no loose ends. But it's too complete. Give me mystery! With the resurrection event, all Christians walk off the map. Beyond that boundary, we rely on faith, not fact, and at this juncture, there is no worse step than to pretend to know what's ahead.

The best plan? Whistle a bit, hold hands, and trust in the Great Maker who made the map in the first place. Here's a bread to make and eat while you journey.

Challah: A Jewish Festival Bread

1. Take 2 level tablespoons of dry yeast, 1 teaspoon of sugar, and ½ cup of warm water, and mix it together. Let it stand for 10 minutes.

2. Put 8 cups of white flour, 2 tablespoons of sugar, and ⅓ cup olive oil, 1 tablespoon of salt in a bowl. Mix in 2½ cups of warm water and 5 eggs.

3. Once yeast is foamy, stir it into the flour mixture and start kneading.

4. Knead for 10 to 15 minutes. (If your dough is still stiff, add a tad more water; a touch more flour if it's still sticking to your hands.)

5. Roll it into a ball and plop it into a greased bread bowl. Then cover with a damp cloth.

6. Two hours later, tip it out onto a floured counter, shape 9 equal balls, and roll them out into 1-inch diameter strands.

7. Braid 3 strands per loaf and place the final braid on a greased cookie sheet.

8. Paint with egg yoke and sprinkle poppy seeds as desired.

9. Allow 2–2½ hours more to rise and bake them at 325°F for 30 to 35 minutes. (Temperature 325°–375°F, depending on your oven.)

This colorful bread is best eaten once it has cooled, but don't let it stand for more than a day. Sweeten it with icing or enjoy it with cheese.

Glossary

Glossary

DOUGH The mixture of flour, water, and yeast—usually requires at least a touch of sugar in order to activate the yeast.

FLOUR (white) White flour is bleached whole wheat flour with the wheat germ, bran, and other particles removed. In most cases, bread at home is made from all-purpose flour, but you can now purchase hard wheat flour or bread flour in some large stores. This will make good firm loaves.

FLOUR (whole wheat) The natural milled wheat containing all the healthy ingredients usually taken out of white flour: bran, wheat germ, etc.

FLOUR (specialty) Some of the recipes in this book call for specialty flours: rye or barley or graham—you can find these in the bulk food section of your grocery store. They're made, as their names suggest, from other grains.

GLAZE There are a number of possibilities here. For a rich brown crust use beaten egg yokes. For a shiny, bright covering, try whipped egg whites. Some people like oil—it gives a softer crust, and water, brushed on several times, will give a thicker, crispier crust.

GREASING THE PAN Make sure the loaf pans are dry—any moisture will cause the grease not to stick, and the loaf will get stubborn at that point. I use shortening (the leftover wax paper is a good greaser), or use soft margarine. Olive oil will also work. The point is to cover it well—not a thick layer, but a thorough covering. Watch the corners especially. This is where dough likes to stick. I don't suggest flouring the greased pan. You'll notice that some recipes call for not greasing the pan, so watch carefully.

KNEADING The practice of working flour and water and yeast into an elastic mass. There is no "correct" way to knead. Most people use the heels of their palms, but you can fold it, pinch it, punch it. Roll it, squish it, play football with it, if you like. The point is to work the dough until the natural gluten turns the sticky mixture into a relatively dry, plastic, and pliable dough. Kneading also works the ingredients evenly throughout the dough. There is no prescribed period of time—anywhere between 10 and 15 minutes will do. I knead until it feels right—if you like music, think of this as three cuts from your favorite CD.

MIXING BOWL You'll want a bowl that has history, if you can find one. My grandmother's blue, ceramic bowl sits in a privileged place in my country kitchen. How many scones she made with it I can never tell. And my own mother used it for pancakes without number. As I use it, all the good wishes from my ancestors get mixed into the dough. There's no rule about the size of bowl, except big. A small bowl may restrict your mixing and spill flour all over. With small children around, you might consider the large metal variety—most superstores have them. They take the beating well. If you do have a metal bowl, place a cloth under it while you do your initial mixing. This will keep the bowl from marking/staining the surface where you will be kneading your dough.

OIL I tend to use to olive oil for all my bread—just to cut back on the cholesterol—but you can use whatever variety you prefer. Certainly for pizza or Italian bread I would prefer olive oil. No oil? You can use shortening or in a pinch, butter. There are a few recipes that call for melted butter—be careful that it cools to warm before you add it to the yeast mixture. For the sweet breakfast breads, you might want to use butter—it adds the "right" scent.

PROOFING THE YEAST This is where most people, if they are going to turn their bread from a light loaf into a solid brick, do the deed. I use the traditional dry yeast (I find the fast-acting kind doesn't give as tasty a flavor). Use warm, not hot water. Stir the sugar into the water first and then sprinkle the yeast on top. Let it stand until it is frothy. This may take anywhere from 7 to 15 minutes. If the yeast is not allowed to proof long enough, it will get mixed into the dough and not rise well. If it touches hot water—either as its proofing or when it's mixed with the flour, it can die out quickly—no yeast, no lift. Jesus said something about that I think (Matthew 13:33).

SALT This is, as Jesus suggested (Matthew 5:13), a key ingredient. The sharper the flavor, the more salt you'll want to use. I add more to pizza dough and less to a sweet bread. A rule of thumb is 1 tablespoon per 8 cups of flour—you won't taste it unless it's not there.

SOUR DOUGH A rising agent that multiplies itself in your fridge or the back of your counter. A home-made leavening agent that gives bread a very specific taste.

SUGAR Even in Italian or French baguettes there is some sugar. It's essential for the yeast to work. I tend to cut it down in white bread and add more to whole wheat bread—to cut the latter's harsh flavor.

WHEAT GERM When wheat is milled, the germ of the kernel can be extracted and used separately as protein—adding it to white flour restores nutritional value without distorting the color greatly. It can be sprinkled onto some flat breads or used as a substitute for cornmeal.

YEAST I prefer the "traditional" active dry yeast. It requires a bit more work than the "instant" version that is introduced right into the dough without proofing. I think there is a significant different in textures and taste. You'll want to check the freshness date—you'll be disappointed if the yeast is past its prime. You can get yeast in packets (one tablespoon per packet) or the cans. Industrial strength bread makers go for the cans.